THE TRIAL OF
ST THOMAS MORE

By the same Author

★

ST THOMAS MORE
ST JOHN FISHER
JOHN SOUTHWORTH
MARGARET ROPER
THREE CARDINALS

Westminster Hall (Courts): Late XVIth c.

The Trial of
St Thomas More

by

E. E. REYNOLDS

P. J. KENEDY & SONS

NEW YORK

First published March 1964
Second impression December 1964

Library of Congress Catalogue Card Number: 63-23059

NIHIL OBSTAT: JOANNES M. T. BARTON, S.T.D., L.S.S., CENSOR DEPUTATUS; IMPRIMATUR:
✠ GEORGIUS L. CRAVEN, EPISCOPUS SEBASTOPOLIS, VIC. CAP.—WESTMONASTERII, DIE 12a
SEPTEMBRIS 1963. THE 'NIHIL OBSTAT' AND 'IMPRIMATUR' ARE A DECLARATION THAT A
BOOK OR PAMPHLET IS CONSIDERED TO BE FREE FROM DOCTRINAL OR MORAL ERROR. IT
IS NOT IMPLIED THAT THOSE WHO HAVE GRANTED THE 'NIHIL OBSTAT' AND 'IMPRIMATUR'
AGREE WITH THE CONTENTS, OPINIONS OR STATEMENTS EXPRESSED. MADE AND PRINTED
IN GREAT BRITAIN. SET IN 'MONOTYPE' BEMBO

CONTENTS

ILLUSTRATIONS

CHIEF REFERENCES

Allen   *Opus Epistolarum Des. Erasmi Roterodami.*
                 Vol. XI.

G & H   *Documents Illustrative of English Church*
                 History, ed. H. Gee and W. J. Hardy.

*Harpsfield**   *Life and Death of Sir Thomas More.*
                 E.E.T.S. (1932).

L.P.   *Letters and Papers of Henry VIII.*

Ordo   *Acta Thomae Mori,* ed. H. de Vocht (1947).

Rogers   *The Correspondence of Sir Thomas More,*
                 ed. E. F. Rogers (1947).

*Roper**   *Life of More.* E.E.T.S. (1935).

Stapleton   *Life of Sir Thomas More,* translated by Mgr
                 P. E. Hallett (1928).

S.P.(S)   State Papers: Spanish.

  * Roper and Harpsfield are now published in one volume in Everyman's Library.

Neither can you be ignorant that those most holy and learned men, John, Bishop of Rochester, and Thomas More, within our memory, for this one and most worthy head of doctrine, the Primacy of the Apostolic See, led the way to martyrdom to many others, to the exceeding glory of the English nation.

St Robert Bellarmine to the Archpriest George Blackwell 28 September 1607

PREFACE

WHEN Father Thomas Bridgett published his *Blessed Thomas More* in 1891, he prefaced it with a careful survey of the authorities on which it was based: More's Works, Erasmus, Roper, Harpsfield, Chauncy [sic], William Rastell, Stapleton, Ro. Ba., Cresacre More, and the State Papers. He was the first biographer of More to make full use of the State Papers. He wrote, 'I have taken nothing at second-hand', and, with regard to *Letters and Papers of Henry VIII*, 'I have sought out the originals in the Record Office or British Museum.' Father Bridgett had indeed made such thorough use of old and new material that his successors have had little to add. R. W. Chambers, for instance, when he came to write his *Thomas More* (1935), declared that Father Bridgett's biography 'can never be superseded'.

Very little new material has come to light since Father Bridgett's day. Professor R. W. Chambers with Dr Elsie Hitchcock and Dr A. W. Reed made a searching examination of the texts of the lives by Roper and Harpsfield, the fruits of which appeared in the Early English Text Society's editions of 1932 and 1935, and of 'Ro.Ba.' in 1950. These studies resulted in a better knowledge of many details both in More's career and in ancillary subjects. Renewed emphasis was also put on the importance of More's own Works, which, Father Bridgett stated, 'have been my principal study'.

Preface

The publication in 1947 of *The Correspondence of Sir Thomas More*, edited by Dr Elizabeth F. Rogers, provided an important aid to further study. In the same year there came from Louvain a volume edited by Professor Henry de Vocht, entitled *Acta Thomae Mori*; this contained the text of another version of More's trial: *Ordo Condemnationis Thomae Mori*. This interesting document will be examined in detail.

Several specialized studies have helped to add to our understanding. In November 1960, Dr J. D. M. Derrett published in the *Bulletin of the Institute of Historical Research* an article entitled 'Neglected Versions of the Contemporary Account of the Trial of Sir Thomas More'. This drew attention to a printed pamphlet of 1536 whose title begins with the word *Novitates*. This, too, will call for examination. Mention should also be made of Mr Geoffrey de C. Parmiter's articles, 'The Indictment of Saint Thomas More' and 'Saint Thomas More and the Oath' in the *Downside Review*, 1959–60. On another aspect there was an article by Dr Margaret Hastings in the *London Guildhall Miscellany* (July 1961) on 'The Ancestry of Sir Thomas More'.

I am glad to draw attention in these pages to a document that has not been previously noted, as far as I can tell. It is the first report to the Council of the conversation between Richard Rich and Sir Thomas More in the Tower. Unfortunately the pages have been spoiled by damp and parts are illegible, but there is a legible passage at the end of some importance. (*See* Appendix.)

This continued interest in all that relates to Sir Thomas More is far from being solely a Catholic concern; indeed, some of the more illuminating contributions have come from those who are not Catholics.

A few indications of this widespread esteem may be noted. There is a University association in Belgium called 'Compagnons de Thomas More'; a Saint Thomas More Exhibition was held in Brussels at the end of 1962. During the Exhibition a small group met to found an international society under the name of 'Amici Thomae Mori'. The Thomas More Society of London was founded in 1928 among lawyers and published two series of papers: *The King's Good Servant* (1948) and *Under God and the Law* (1949). For some years there has also been a Thomas More Society in the United States of America. The most notable development, however, is the Saint Thomas More Project of Yale University under the chairmanship of Professor Louis L. Martz, with Professor Richard S. Sylvester as executive editor. The purpose is to publish the complete works, Latin and English. Two series have been planned. The first is a scholarly edition in twelve volumes, and the second a popular edition in seven volumes. Publication of both series has begun. A *Preliminary Bibliography* edited by R. W. Gibson was published at Yale in 1961.

The welcome given on both sides of the Atlantic to Mr Robert Bolt's notable play, *A Man for All Seasons* (1961), is yet another indication of the extensive appeal made by St Thomas More to men and women of various kinds of belief or of no defined belief.

It may also be recorded that a Member of Parliament tabled the following motion in the House of Commons on 14 March 1963:

That this House, mindful of past members and others who have suffered persecution for conscience' sake, and recalling the exemplary profession of Mr Speaker More (Subsequently Lord High Chancellor of England) that he died the King's good servant but God's first, is of the opinion that the dictum of the Lord Chief Justice of England, to the effect that a good citizen puts the interests of the State above everything, is unacceptable unless so qualified as to remove its totalitarian implication.

Is it possible to explain this increasing interest in St Thomas More? I think part of the answer is given in the Preface to the printed edition of Mr Bolt's play. He stated that he himself was not 'in the meaningful sense of the word a Christian', and asked, 'So by what right do I appropriate a Christian Saint to my purpose?' More was not prepared to surrender the inner citadel of his being, his conscience as he termed it, by taking an oath with his tongue in his cheek. As Mr Bolt writes, 'A man takes an oath only when he wants to commit himself quite exceptionally to the statement, when he wants to make an identity between the truth of it and his own virtue; he offers himself as a guarantee. And it works.' To More an oath was 'not merely a time-honoured and understood ritual but also a definite contract'. It was this refusal to sacrifice self, 'selfhood' to use Mr Bolt's term, that makes More so important today. We may put this in a political context. The smashing of Nazism in Germany and of Fascism in Italy did not, alas, bring to an end that twentieth-century aberration known as totalitarianism—a word as ugly as the thinking behind it. As Communism or as military domination it is to be found in control of large sections of the world; some of the countries that have achieved independence since the war have lost the independence of citizenship under military rule. 'Selfhood' has been suppressed and those who dare to assert their individual views have suffered forced labour, torture and an ugly death. Those of us who live under more liberal conditions are unconsciously influenced by this continuous pressure of a hostile political view of life. Ideas are not confined to national boundaries; they travel without passports; if they are evil, they must be resisted. It is therefore not surprising that we find inspiration and renewed courage in the example set four centuries ago by St Thomas More.

Mr Bolt rightly emphasizes how much More had to sacrifice. Few men have led such full and satisfying lives; he reached the head of his profession; for a period he had the confidence of the King. He was a man of culture whose friendship was sought by scholars of other countries. He was happiest in his lively family circle. As Mr Bolt says, 'He parted with more than most men when he parted with his life.'

All these things are true yet they are not the full story nor do they reach the source of his strength—his religious faith and his complete trust in God. There is an interesting parallel with the widespread popularity of St Francis of Assisi in the early years of this century. G. K. Chesterton pointed out that people admired St Francis for all manner of good reasons, and it is possible to write of him 'almost without raising any religious questions at all. In short, he [the biographer] may try to tell the story of a saint without God; which is like being told to write the life of Nansen and forbidden to mention the North Pole.' Now, the study of More's trial is valuable because, after his condemnation, he at last spoke his mind. He did not die for a legal quibble; he died in defence of what he knew was an essential element of the Catholic Church. To quote G.K.C. again, 'It will remain a permanent and determining fact, a hinge of history, that he saw, in that first hour of madness, that Rome and Reason are one. He saw at the very beginning, what so many have now only begun to see at the end: that the real hopes of learning and liberty lay in preserving the Roman unity of Europe and the ancient Christian loyalty for which he died.'

In view of this increasing interest in St Thomas More and of the new studies that have been made of particular aspects of his life, it seemed to me useful to make an extended examination of his trial, more detailed than is possible in a one-volume biography.

This has also given me the opportunity to correct or amplify one or two statements in my *Saint Thomas More* and *Margaret Roper*.

Chapter 1

THE EARLIEST RECORDS

THE Indictment is the earliest document on the trial, as it shows its scope; it will, however, be better to consider this separately at a later stage. Here we are concerned with the earliest narratives of the course of the trial.

I. THE PARIS NEWS LETTER

This convenient name has been given to the earliest known account of the trial of Sir Thomas More. There are eight manuscript copies in the Bibliothèque Nationale in Paris.[1] The word 'copies' should be noted; the author's autograph manuscript is not extant. The copies we have, or, sometimes, copies of copies, are liable to all the errors that creep into even the most carefully written manuscripts. Such errors may be due to carelessness, or misreadings, or, where a copy is being used, to repetition of previous errors. Other deviations may be caused when the copyist 'improves' his copy, either by thinking that he knows better than his predecessor or because he adds a bit of information that comes his way or embroiders with a touch of his own imagination. Our strict rules of transcription were unknown in the sixteenth century and for long afterwards. From this it will be seen how difficult it is to produce a

---

[1] For a carefully collated text see *Harpsfield*, pp. 258–66. The relationship of the manuscripts is discussed there on p. 257.

version that is absolutely reliable. Of the copies of the *News Letter*, only one seems to have been made from the original; the others are at one or more removes from it. One copy is dated 4 August 1535, but it is defective; six other copies were done in the sixteenth century and one is of the early seventeenth century. All make the curious mistake of giving Wednesday, 7 July, as the day of the execution, whereas it was Tuesday, 6 July.[1] They give the correct date of the trial, 1 July.

The account is concerned solely with More's trial, and, very briefly, with his execution. There is no reference to the trials and executions of the Carthusians and their fellow martyrs. The only mention of John Fisher comes in the report of More's remarks at his own trial. The author would be anxious to get his report circulated as soon as possible as the concern about the fate of Thomas More was widespread, more widespread than that for the fate of John Fisher. Presumably the author had no certain news of Fisher's trial, which had taken place a fortnight earlier.

Who was the writer of this report? There is no hint in the *News Letter* of his identity, nor of the source of his information. It is a matter of speculation whether he himself was at the trial, or whether, as some scholars think, he was passing on the contents of a report he had received from someone coming from London, or that had been brought by a traveller. It may be that the observer at the trial, whoever he was, at once left England and the *News Letter* records a verbal report he made to a friend on his

[1] This error was not unique. The Emperor's ambassador in England, Eustace Chapuys, gives the date of execution as the 5th July in a letter dated 11 July (*L.P.*, vol. 8, No. 1019).

arrival in Paris, or, as this seems just as likely to me, he himself wrote the *News Letter*. Some of the variations that occur in the copies and translations may be explained by the kind of errors and misreadings just mentioned. An imperfect knowledge of English could account for some awkward phrases.

It has been argued that the first account was written in Latin. 'The *News Letter*', Mr J. D. M. Derrett has written, 'is evidently a very close translation of a Latin original . . . and in the process of translation some cryptic and laconic phrases of the Latin have given rise to mistakes.'[1] There is no hint in contemporary records of such a Latin version having existed, and it does seem strange that such an important document vanished apparently within a matter of weeks. Moreover, as we shall see, the most important translation of the *News Letter* was made into Latin. This was the *Expositio* printed at Basle in the autumn of 1535; at the end the translator or editor stated that he was writing from Paris on 23 July 1535, and there is no reason to set aside such a definite statement. One would have thought that at such an early date (a fortnight after the execution) the presumed Latin original would still have been available, so why translate the French back into Latin? The time factor must be taken into account. Assuming that the traveller left London on the day of the execution (6 July) it would take him at least a week or ten days to get to Paris under the most favourable conditions of wind and weather and relays of horses. He would get to Paris not earlier than, perhaps, the 14th July. The presumed

[1] *Bulletin of the Institute of Historical Research*, November 1960, pp. 202–23. References to Mr Derrett are to this article.

Latin report would then have to be translated into French, followed by a translation back into Latin. This is not impossible, but it suggests quick work. The hypothesis of a Latin original may explain some variations in the texts, but it does not solve all problems.

The *Paris News Letter* is the key document for our knowledge of the trial.

II. THE EXPOSITIO

Two German translations of the *News Letter* were printed in 1535 and a third in 1536. The most important translation was into Latin and was printed by Jerome Froben at Basle early in October 1535. It was entitled *Expositio fidelis de morte D. Thomae Mori et quorundam aliorum insignium virorum in Anglia*. It was headed 'P.M. CASPARIA GRIP. S.D.', i.e. as a letter from P.M. to Caspar Agrippinensis. Nothing certain is known of this Caspar unless he can be identified with the Gaspar who visited Erasmus at Basle in the summer of 1535 and then left for Cologne with letters of introduction from Erasmus.[1] This edition was reprinted at Antwerp in 1536. It was later included as a supplementary document in the Latin works of More published at Basle in 1563 by F. Episcopius, who was the son of N. Episcopius (Bischoff), the partner of Jerome Froben. The letter was then headed 'G. COURINUS NUCERINUS PHIL.MONT. S.D.' The original publication of 1535 is more likely to be correct than an edition published twenty-eight years later; how the change came about cannot be satisfactorily explained. Courinus had been amanuensis to

---

[1] The editors of *Allen*, No 3041, suggest that this Gaspar may have been Gaspar Schets.

Erasmus until he left Basle in October 1535 to take up his benefice as canon of Nozeroy (Jura). It may be that Episcopius recalled that Courinus had had something to do with the 1535 production; he may have been using the original manuscript copied out by Courinus which lacked the printed ascription. The value of the new printing was that it expanded 'P.M.' to 'Phil.Mont.' and thus leads to the name of Philip Montanus (perhaps the Latinized 'Dumont', or 'Montaigne'). We shall return to him presently.

The best text of the *Expositio* is given as an Appendix to *Allen*. The 460 lines there can be divided as follows:

1–28. An introductory paragraph followed by a brief account of the topography of London.

29–210. The translation of the *Paris News Letter*.

211–286. A summary account of the trials and executions of the Carthusians, Richard Reynolds and Bishop John Fisher.

287–460. Some reflections on these events, especially on the death of More. The point of view is given in the sentence, 'I would have liked the King to show less severity, and the victims not to defy the storm openly.'

The section following the *News Letter* begins: 'What I have so far recorded is for the most part given in a statement circulated by hand among people in Paris. Whoever wrote it must have been present on the occasion. What follows is derived partly from friends' letters and partly from hearsay.' This makes it clear that the passage from line 29 to 210 is a translation of the *News Letter*, which, he implies, was written by an observer at the trial. It may also have been printed, but no copy has survived. He

5

did not know, or did not give, the name of the writer.

What part did Philip Montanus play in this? He was a Frenchman who, after his studies in Paris, went to Basle and became a pupil-secretary to Erasmus. The closeness of the friendship that developed between them is shown by the legacy from Erasmus of 150 crowns. Montanus returned to Paris in the summer of 1528 and became a noted tutor of Greek. He remained there until 1562, when he became Rector of Queen's College in the University of Douai. He had therefore been in a position to learn the details of More's trial when these were received in Paris and he would know how anxiously Erasmus waited for news of his friend's fate and he would therefore hasten to send a report to Basle, putting it into Latin as Erasmus had little knowledge of French.

It was long assumed that Erasmus himself was responsible for the *Expositio*, but the editors of *Allen* reject this ascription.[1] It may be noted that F. Episcopius did not name Erasmus as the author. The introductory paragraph on the topography of London has been used as an argument in favour of Erasmus, but the information given was slight. The Latinity of the last portion is certainly not of Erasmian standard. He may well have proposed the compilation of the *Expositio* and have suggested its form, and the ideas expressed in the final commentary. The attitude there taken is in keeping with the view of Erasmus given in a letter written on 24 August 1535[2] before he had received definite news of More's execution. He wrote: 'Would that he had never embroiled himself in this perilous business and had

---

[1] This matter will be further considered when we discuss the *Ordo*.
[2] *Allen*, No 3048.

left theological questions to the theologians.' He was certainly not the author of the part incorporating the *News Letter* and a passage in the second part rules him out unless, as has been suggested, he was carrying out an elaborate scheme of deception. The passage reads: 'With the Carthusians there was Reginald [Reynolds] a Brigettine monk, a man of angelic countenance and spirit, and of sound judgment, with whom I had some conversation when I visited England in the train of Cardinal Campeggio.' Campeggio was in England in 1518 and again from October 1528 to October 1529 on the Divorce business; the reference seems more likely to be to the second occasion than to the first. It should be noted that Campeggio and Erasmus had formed a friendship during the three years (1506–9) that Erasmus was in Italy and they kept in correspondence. Anyone recommended to Campeggio by Erasmus would be sure of a welcome. The mention of Richard Reynolds is even more interesting. He took his B.D. at Cambridge in 1513, when he was also University preacher under the scheme established by Bishop John Fisher as Chancellor. Erasmus was at Cambridge from August 1511 to January 1514 as lecturer in Greek. As Reynolds became a recognized master of Latin, Greek and Hebrew, the two must have known each other in what was a small society; the link would be Greek. In 1513 Reynolds entered the Brigettine monastery of Syon at Isleworth in Middlesex, a step that Erasmus would probably not approve. His fame as a classical scholar and theologian grew with the years. Among his friends was Thomas More, who frequently visited Syon. Erasmus described Reynolds as 'a well-known and distinguished scholar'.[1] It may be suggested that the member of Campeggio's suite who visited Reynolds was himself a scholar who wanted to meet a leading English scholar known to Erasmus. He could have been Philip Montanus, who might have come to England at some period during the year of Campeggio's mission and, as a protégé of Erasmus, have secured the Cardinal's protection by being temporarily attached to his suite. Montanus as a prominent Greek scholar may have wished to meet Reynolds; no doubt he would also meet More and other friends of Erasmus.

The *Expositio* ends with the statement that it was sent from Paris on 23 July 1535, though that date may refer only to the part based on the *News Letter*. So the picture we can draw is of Montanus sending a translation of the *News Letter* to Erasmus (though we must not exclude the possibility that he sent the French version which was translated at Basle) and adding to it what he had gathered from letters, while recalling his meeting with Richard Reynolds. This account may have been adapted for publication with some additional comments; it was then prepared for the press by his amanuensis Courinus. When, nearly thirty years later, F. Episcopius came to include it in the Latin works of More, his recollection of what happened may have been vague save for the fact that Courinus had had something to do with it. This suggestion, admittedly conjectural, has the merit of accepting the ascription, place

---

[1] *Allen*, No 3056. There is a difficulty here, as so often with Erasmus. In his letter, dated 12 September 1535, he wrote 'Reginaldus Polus' following the names of Fisher and More. As the editors of *Allen* say, 'It is hardly conceivable that he should have supposed Pole [who was then in Italy] to have been martyred at the same time as Fisher and More.' Having written 'Reginaldus' the old man's pen slipped into adding 'Polus'.

and date as printed in the Basle edition, and there seems no valid reason for thinking these were deliberate deceptions.

It will be of interest at this point to trace how the news of More's execution reached Erasmus as far as extant documents tell the tale. The first report came from Conrad Goclenius in a letter dated 10 August 1535, probably from Louvain, as the writer was then Professor of Latin there. He wrote: 'Thomas More was executed in Britain on the 6 July,[1] showing himself no less steadfast in his trial and execution than did Socrates before his infamous Athenian prosecutors. The Bishop of Rochester was put to death a few days earlier against whom the King's anger was increased because he had been made a Cardinal.' He gave as the reason for More's condemnation his refusal to accept the King as Supreme Head of the English Church, his contention that the King's marriage with Catherine of Aragon was lawful, and his correspondence in the Tower with Fisher. This was an admirable summary of the main points. Goclenius added, 'As soon as I get more definite news, I will let you know.' He added a few details in a letter dated 28 September.

The next reference is in a letter written from Cologne by Tielmann Gravius on 17 August. 'I deeply deplore', he wrote, 'the unhappy fate of the Bishop of Rochester and of Thomas More.' The only detail he added was wrong. 'Both were executed on London Bridge in sight of the populace.' A letter of the same date from Antwerp written

---

[1] The Latin reads 'sexto nonas Julii' and the editors of *Allen* and others give this as 2 July. It has been pointed out by Mr J. D. M. Derrett (*op. cit.*) that 'it was the habit at this period to write *quinto nonas* or *sexto nonas* for the 5th and 6th of a month where the nones occurred on the 7th.'

by Erasmus Schets, a merchant-banker, contains a bare reference to the executions.

Erasmus did not write at length on the loss of More,[1] but in a letter to the Bishop of Cracow, Peter Tomiczki, dated 31 August, he said: 'From the extract I enclose from a letter you will learn of the fate of the Bishop of Rochester and Thomas More, than whom England never had two men more saintly or more learned. I feel as if I had died with More so closely were our two souls united.' The extract he sent was probably from Goclenius's letter of 10 August just quoted, though there is the possibility that, as he had promised, Goclenius had later sent a fuller account that has been lost.

In the middle of December, Erasmus acknowledged receiving from Damien a Goes an account of the deaths of Fisher and More written in Italian by Cardinal Pole. Erasmus wrote: 'I do not understand Italian but I will arrange for the translation of what Pole has translated.'[2] This account, or translation, by Pole is not extant; it may have been an independent account; had it been a translation or expansion of the *News Letter*, Erasmus would surely have recognized it. It may be noted that on 6 October, Dr Pedro Ortiz, the Emperor's Proctor, sent from Rome 'a copy of the passion and martyrdom' of More.[3] Perhaps this was a translation of the *News Letter* (there is no reference to Fisher) or Pole's account.

---

[1] *Harpsfield*, p. 255, ascribes to Erasmus a set of verses beginning 'Extinctum flamus', but de Vocht (*Ordo*, p. 196) has shown that they were by the poet Janus Secundus, Imperial Secretary.

[2] For letters referred to in the last four paragraphs, see *Allen*, Nos 3037, 3041, 3042, 3049, 3061, 3076.

[3] *S.P.(S).*, 5, i, No 208.

III. THE ORDO

We now come to a puzzling document discovered by Professor Henry de Vocht of Louvain about 1934, but not published until 1947. It is headed:

Ordo Condemnationis Thomae Mori, Cancellarii Primarii Ali-quando Regni Angliae, quia in incestas nuptias Henrici Octavi assentiri, eumque caput summum Ecclesie Anglicanae fateri noluerit: compendio latine redditus: anno illoquo ille perierat.

(The course of the condemnation of Thomas More, once first chancellor of England, because he would not assent to the adulterous marriage of Henry VIII, nor acknowledge him as Supreme Head of the English Church: in the year in which he suffered.)

The first point to make is that the words 'in the year in which he suffered' were added at a later date than that on which the manuscript was written. The *Ordo* was put together by Gerard Morinck, who died in 1556. He was a theologian at Louvain and had known Goclenius (d. 1539). All we can be sure of is that this account was written between 1535 and 1556. Unfortunately de Vocht was so excited at his discovery that he allowed his imagination to run away with him and he propounded a theory of the origin of the *Ordo* that strains credulity. Confidence in his judgment is shaken by a number of errors of fact in his argument. Some of them are still repeated by those who have not troubled to keep up to date with the results of research during this century.

A footnote on page 29 reads: 'Thomas More's head was procured [sic] from London Bridge to Margaret Roper; it was placed in her arms after her death and buried with her in St Dunstan's Church, Canterbury.' She was buried in the More vault in Chelsea Old Church; it is said that she left her father's head to her eldest daughter Elizabeth, Lady Bray; at some time after her death (1558) it was placed in the Roper vault at St Dunstan's, Canterbury. It was still there, in a niche behind a grille, when the vault was accidentally opened last century.[1]

Another example of how difficult it is to kill old tales is given on page 72, where it is implied that Erasmus 'resided as a guest at Chelsea House'. Erasmus left England for the last time in April 1517 and it was not until 1523 or 1524 that More went to Chelsea to live. On the same page it is said that Erasmus was 'intimately acquainted' with Margaret More (Roper); she was not more than eleven years old when Erasmus last left England. The *Expositio* adds this description of her to the account given in the *News Letter*: 'a woman of exceptional grace of figure combined with great dignity of bearing, resembling her father in discernment, manners and learning.' That is not the memory Erasmus carried away of a girl of eleven. It must have been written by someone who saw her as a woman; this could have been the visitor who sought out Richard Reynolds. We must regard it as yet another elusive clue to the authorship of the *Expositio*.

On page 38 it is said that Erasmus was 'acquainted' with English and could therefore read the report that de Vocht predicates was written in English. Erasmus did not know any contemporary language other than his native Dutch. We have seen that he acknowledged that he could not read

---

[1] *See* below, Chapter 13. That she was buried at Chelsea is stated in William Roper's will. See my *Margaret Roper*, p. 140.

even Italian, although he had spent three years in Italy; nor did he trouble to learn English during his residence in England, nor French while in France. No doubt he picked up enough vocabulary to speak to servants, but his intercourse was with scholars and Latin was their medium. De Vocht also makes much of the knowledge of London and England shown in the *Expositio* and *Ordo*, but it is very elementary. Thus the paragraph in the *Expositio* on London really says little more than that the Tower was at one end and Westminster at the other.

A more serious error is made about the 'pensions' Erasmus received from England; this is used by de Vocht to support his contention that Erasmus wrote the *Expositio*. According to the argument, the comment in the last part was purposely restrained in tone, as Erasmus feared his 'pensions' would be stopped if he criticized Henry VIII's policy. It is true that he had always been cautious in any statements published over his name; he was 'of the willow not the oak'. This did not prevent him from making outright criticisms anonymously; when charged with their authorship he either evaded the question or blandly denied responsibility. The matter of the 'pensions' has a simpler explanation. It may be first noted that Erasmus had never had a pension from Henry VIII, as de Vocht implies on page 56. Erasmus was given two livings, one at Aldington in Kent and another of which the name is not known. Archbishop Warham had arranged for £20 a year to be paid to Erasmus out of Aldington. The vicar was Richard Master, and Aldington was the parish in which Elizabeth Barton, the Nun of Kent, was born and had her first visions. When she and her associates were arrested early in

1534, Richard Master was also arrested. They were all attaindered; Master was pardoned, but the others were hanged at Tyburn. One result was that Master lost his living and his goods and could no longer pay Erasmus his share of the income. Erasmus was annoyed at this loss and wrote to his friends in England to get their help.[1] In the end Thomas Cromwell and his jackal, Thomas Bedyll, clerk of the Council, had the money sent. No doubt Cromwell thought it wise to keep the aged scholar in good humour lest he should rouse European opinion on the subject of More's death; in fact horror at the execution was widespread without any help from Erasmus. We have to admit that Erasmus became more and more concerned about money in his old age, and, like others who have suffered penury in youth, he thought he was poor; actually he left a comfortable fortune. This may have put some restraint on him, but it does not justify de Vocht's argument that Erasmus covered up his authorship of the *Expositio* by an elaborate series of subterfuges such as using the names of Philip Montanus, Courinus, and others, and, one may add, by writing in indifferent Latin.

Erasmus paid tribute to Fisher and More in the Preface to *Ecclesiastes* (1535), a book on the art of preaching which he had proposed dedicating to Fisher. He was an old man of about seventy when he returned to Basle from Freiburg in June 1535 and became the guest of Jerome Froben. His intention was to supervise some printing and to wind up his affairs and then, in the spring, to go down the Rhine to pass his remaining years near his native land. Increasing

[1] In happier days he had troubled Thomas More to see that the pension came punctually; e.g. *see, Allen,* Nos 388, 467, 481, 499.

feebleness of health prevented the plan from being carried out, and for much of his twelve months in Basle he was bedridden. We cannot doubt the sincerity of his grief at the death of Thomas More. 'I feel as if I had died with More so closely were our two souls united.' Perhaps had he been in his full strength he would have written at greater length about his lost friend. As it was he died almost exactly a year after Thomas More.

Professor de Vocht evolved a complicated story to connect the *Ordo* and the *Expositio*. Briefly his theory was this: the *Ordo* is a translation of an account in English (now lost) of the trial written by More's nephew William Rastell; this he sent to Goclenius, who passed it on to Erasmus, who in his turn wrote a first Latin version (now lost) based on Rastell's account, and claimed, to cover himself, that it was from a correspondent in Paris; this first *Expositio* was translated into French (the *News Letter*) and also into German and Spanish. Later Erasmus published an expanded edition of the first *Expositio*, and it is this second and later version that we now know under that title. The *Ordo* is claimed to be the closest version available of the lost Rastell report to Goclenius. This too ingenious theory raises more problems than it solves. It depends on two lost documents and even one lost document should not be postulated unless the evidence is compulsive. It is easy to suggest that a crucial document has been lost in order to explain difficulties that are created by lack of material. De Vocht's main assumption, that William Rastell wrote an account in 1535 of his uncle's trial, has little to support it. There is no hint anywhere that he was present at the trial. None of the More family is recorded as having been present. The fact that the King gave permission for them to attend the burial implies that they were not allowed to be present at the trial and execution. Apart from that, it strains belief to be asked to assume that had any one of them been present Roper or Harpsfield would not have said so and used their recollections. As we shall see, Roper stated that he himself was not there (though an official of the King's Bench Court), but he carefully named his authorities.

It is also difficult to see why Rastell should have sent an account of the trial to Goclenius; had he written such an account he was more likely to send it to Erasmus and to have written it in Latin, rather than to someone whose connection with Thomas More was slight. De Vocht assumed, without any evidence, that Goclenius sent a full account of the trial to Erasmus in fulfilment of his promise in his letter of 10 August. In brief, de Vocht's theory assumes too much, but this does not lessen the importance of the *Ordo*. It is unfortunate that we cannot be sure of the date of its composition. My own impression is that it is an account written up from what information the author could gather; this would include the *Expositio*. He did not slavishly copy his authorities but worked the whole into an original composition and in doing so added a few speculative passages of his own or incorporated rumoured accounts of the trial.

IV. NOVITATES

Mr J. D. M. Derrett has drawn attention to this Latin pamphlet bearing the date 24 April 1536.[1] Much material

[1] Mr Derrett acknowledged his own indebtedness to Dr H. G. Richardson.

has been condensed into these twenty-one small pages. First comes an account of the trial of Richard Reynolds and the Carthusians; three pages are given to the defence Reynolds made and another three to the Carthusians, with an account of the executions. Half a page, with a reference to Bishop John Fisher, leads to an eight-page description of the trial and execution of Thomas More. Then comes a copy of a Brief dated 22 July 1535 from the Pope to Ferdinand, King of the Romans,[1] occupying three and a half pages. The pamphlet ends with two pages containing three fourteen-line pasquils, the first to the King of France warning him to beware of the English, the second to the Emperor Charles V urging him to beware of a change in his fortunes, and the third to both of them begging them to cease fighting each other and to combine to fight the Turks.

This pamphlet, probably printed in Germany (Cologne?), bears no indications of its authorship. It was apparently intended as a denunciation of Henry VIII's treatment of those who opposed his will and chose to remain loyal to the Apostolic See. The materials were well selected. The defence Richard Reynolds made at his trial with the Carthusians is a clear statement of the position he and others

---

One undated copy is in the Cock Collection at the London Guildhall and another in the Bodleian. Two dated copies are in the British Museum; this edition appeared before the undated ones, as the latter make use of the errata printed at the end of the 1536 edition.

[1] King of the Romans from 1531; succeeded his brother, Charles V, as Emperor, in 1588. A similar Brief to Francis I of France, dated 26 July 1535, is printed in Pierre Janelle's edition of Gardiner's writings in *Obedience in Church and State* (Cambridge, 1930), which contains Gardiner's reply, 'Si sedes illa Romana.'

felt compelled to take up. 'I have all the rest of Christendom in my favour,' he said in objecting to the Act of Supremacy—an argument echoed by Thomas More. Prior Houghton's pertinent question to Cromwell is then given, 'How could the King, being a layman, be Head of the Church?' The execution of the Carthusians with Richard Reynolds and John Haile is then briefly recorded. A connecting passage refers to others, including 'John, Cardinal and Bishop of Rochester, Thomas More, Chancellor to the King, many Carthusians and secular priests' who were faithful unto death. This brings the writer, or compiler, to the account of the trial and execution of Thomas More. The Papal Brief to Ferdinand deplored the death of Cardinal Fisher; his promotion as Cardinal was intended to protect him; Henry VIII had acted more impiously than Henry II; he should be deprived of his kingdom and the aid of Ferdinand and other princes was sought to carry out this decision. The fate of Thomas More was probably not yet known in Rome. It will be seen that these three chapters, as they may be called, are closely connected. The three pasquils at the end are less relevant.

These accounts of Reynolds, the Carthusians, Fisher and More follow, or are followed by, the narratives ascribed to the London Carthusian monk Maurice Chauncy. This ascription can now be definitely set aside, as Chauncy was not in a position to write the accounts printed in *Novitates* in 1536, and it may be that someone collecting accounts of the Henrician martyrs brought together these records with Chauncy's main narrative of the Carthusians, *Historia aliquot saeculi martyrum Anglorum* (1550), which was written not earlier than 1546, when Chauncy (who, to his lasting regret, had taken the oath) had found refuge in Bruges.[1] In the Record Office there is a transcript of an account in Italian in the Vatican Archives of the defence made by Reynolds, of Prior Houghton's questions and of the executions. An English translation is given in *L.P.*, Vol. 8, No 661. There is no clue as to the origin of this account; could it be connected with the Italian narrative by Pole? There is another copy of the narratives at the London Guildhall compiled about 1560.

Though the accounts of the trials of Reynolds and the Carthusians do not directly bear upon that of Thomas More, they have an interest that will excuse a digression. There are variations in the versions. The Vatican manuscript correctly gives the date of the Carthusians' trial as 28 April; *Novitates* and *Anon.*[2] give 15 April. Neither account makes it clear that the main statement by Reynolds was made on the day of the trial (28th), and that his words beginning 'This is of the things of this world' were spoken after judgment had been given on the following day (29th). The next paragraph in each account is chronologically out of order. Prior Houghton's question was put to the commissioners either in the Tower or at some earlier date; this was not part of the trial, and Chauncy in his *Historia* does not mention the interview. The Vatican manuscript speaks of 'the Prior of the Grande Chartreuse of Flanders', a most curious error. *Novitates* and *Anon.* correct this and give the name of 'the Prior of the London

[1] A list of the Latin editions of the narratives is given on pp. 346–8 of E. M. Thompson, *The Carthusian Order in England* (1930). To her list must now be added *Novitates*, and Guildhall MS 1231.

[2] *Anon.* is here used as a convenient reference to the four pieces printed with Chauncy's *Historia* in 1550.

Carthusians, John Houghton'. The Vatican manuscript has, 'The Prior . . . went to the King's Almoner[1] and two other doctors.' *Novitates* (both editions) names one of the doctors as 'Latinet', but *Anon.* gives 'Latimer', which seems more likely, as Hugh Latimer (later Bishop of Worcester) was employed on other inquiries of this kind at that period.

It is impossible to be sure of the relationship between *Novitates* and *Anon.* Apart from errors of fact noted and some verbal variations, they closely resemble one another and the *Expositio*. Chauncy could have used *Novitates* sometime after his arrival in Bruges in 1546 or 1547, but, as has been pointed out, it is improbable that he had anything to do with the copies that have been ascribed to him. His task was to record the story of his own monastery. There would have been no point in producing separately the very brief and inadequate account of the Carthusians given in *Novitates*.

What is the relationship between all these narratives? No completely satisfactory answer can be given for lack of essential data, but that does not rule out profitable speculation.

We have considered four (or five if we include *Anon.*) contemporary or near-contemporary accounts. The *News Letter*, the *Expositio*, the *Ordo*, and *Novitates* all deal with the same subject-matter and they were bound to have much in common, but the relationship is closer than that between narratives written by different people about one event. The wording is so similar that it suggests a common

[1] Edward Foxe, later Bishop of Hereford, who had been much employed in the divorce business.

source either direct or at second-hand. There is, however, a striking similarity, though a negative one, that should be noted. We shall find when we come to examine William Roper's account of the trial that he added the More-Rich interview to what had previously been recorded. This alone suggests that the other accounts relied on a common source; this does not rule out the possibility of the *News Letter* being the parent document, even though we have only copies (early ones, it is true) of it; the vagaries and personal feelings of copyists can account for many a discrepancy.

It is not necessary to extend our previous discussions of Professor de Vocht's theory about the *Ordo*. Sufficient has been said to reject it as too speculative to win support. The genealogy he proposed was as follows: his imagined but lost Rastell report was the primary source. From this were derived directly the first but also lost *Expositio*, written by Erasmus, and the *Ordo*. From this first *Expositio* came the second (printed at Basle), the *News Letter* and the German and Spanish translations.

A more reasonable suggestion has been made by Mr J. D. M. Derrett in his article to which reference has already been made. According to this, the *News Letter, Novitates* and the *Ordo* were based on an account in Latin which has been lost. From the *News Letter* are derived the printed *Expositio* and the other translations, and from these *Anon.*

This is a well-argued scheme of relationship. Mr Derrett has added a reconstructed Latin text that repays careful study; this is not put forward as the lost original, but as a suggestion of the material out of which the existing narratives were shaped. This seems to me a possible solution of the problem of source, but I should be inclined to think that the *News Letter* is the starting-point of existing narratives; nor would I place the *Ordo* as near the source as he and Professor de Vocht have done. It contains elements that suggest a somewhat later compilation in which the writer clarified what seemed obscure to him and added some material that had come his way or that he thought should be included. A number of details will be considered when we come to discuss the trial itself.

It would not be surprising if other hitherto unknown versions, such as *Novitates*, came to light. Anonymous pamphlets tend to lurk in old libraries and unsuspected places. What would be surprising, yet most welcome, would be an account of the trial that adds anything significant to the *News Letter*. These various versions are a notable tribute to the widespread regard shown for Sir Thomas More; by contrast, the interest taken in the trial and fate of Bishop John Fisher was meagre, a fact that is as true today as in the sixteenth century.

Chapter 2

LATER ACCOUNTS

I. ROPER

WILLIAM ROPER (1495?–1578) wrote his account of the life of Sir Thomas More about 1556. It was first published in 1626 with the title *The Mirrour of Vertue in Worldly Greatness*. It bore the false imprint of Paris, whereas it had been printed at the English College Press at St Omer. Roper did not plan his memoir as a book, but wrote down his recollections to help Nicholas Harpsfield (1519–75), who had undertaken to write a biography of Sir Thomas More. This explains the omission of some matters from Roper's account; there is, for instance, no reference to More's books and controversies; even *Utopia* is not mentioned, though Ralph Robinson's translation had appeared in 1551. When Roper came to record the trial, he confined himself to supplying what was lacking from the *News Letter* and the *Expositio*—the evidence of Rich.

Roper was writing at least twenty years after the trial; this inevitably gives his record less authority than it would have had if written down in 1535. It has sometimes been hinted that, as he was about sixty years of age in 1556, his memory may have been unreliable, but the very sharp pictures that are given in the memoir of events that happened before 1535 show that there was no vagueness in his recollections. Moreover, as he was active in the law for another twenty years it can safely be assumed that there was no loss of intellectual alertness. There are, of course, some errors, but none of serious importance.[1] It may be well to remind ourselves that verbatim reports of things said were almost unknown at that period; writers put down as accurately as they could what they remembered and sometimes they adopted the classical method of inventing speeches to fit the occasion. These would convey the true force of what was said, provided the recorder had some sense of responsibility, but they did not come near our standard of accurate reporting.

We may first note Roper's personal advantages as a reporter of the trial. His father, John, was Clerk of the Pleas, or Prothonotary, in the King's Bench Court, and his will, dated 27 January 1524, shows that his son William then held the office conjointly; after his father's death he continued as Prothonotary until his own death in 1578. For some years he shared the office with Richard Heywood. The point to note is that few men could have been more familiar with procedure in the King's Bench. His marriage with Margaret More in 1521 and their residence with her father until his arrest in 1534 meant that he would know as much as anyone in the More household of the course of events, and they must have made every effort to get reliable information about the trial. Roper was careful to name some of his authorities.

This much touching Sir Thomas More's arraignment, being not thereat present myself, have I by credible report,

---

[1] They are given in *Roper*, pp. xlvi–xlvii.

partly of the right worshipful Sir Anthony St Leger, knight, and partly of Richard Heywood and John Webbe, gentlemen, with others of good credit, at the hearing thereof present themselves, as far as my poor wit and memory would serve me, here truly rehearsed unto you.

Anthony St Leger (1496?–1559) was born at Ulcombe, Kent, and was educated at Cambridge and Gray's Inn. At the time of More's trial he was in the service of Thomas Cromwell; he managed to adjust himself to the changes in religion, though he was reputed to be papistically inclined. His brother was Prior of Leeds (Augustinian), in Kent, until its surrender. Sir Anthony, as he became, spent the last three years of his life at Ulcombe after having spent some years in Ireland as an efficient Lord Deputy. Only one fact has been discovered about John Webbe. In 1547 William Roper and William Rastell leased Crosby Place from Antonio Bonvisi, More's old friend. Two months later Bonvisi conveyed the property in trust to Richard Heywood and John Webbe. This suggests that John Webbe was a lawyer. In 1549 Bonvisi left the country for Louvain, where he was joined by other members of the More circle, the Clements and Rastells. A year later they were joined by a former Fellow of New College, Oxford, Nicholas Harpsfield. In spite of the legal arrangements made by Bonvisi to safeguard his property, Crosby Place was seized by the City Sheriffs, but Roper, Heywood, and Webbe seem to have continued their tenancy.

Of the three names given by Rastell, that of Richard Heywood is the most significant. He was a law student at the time of the trial and later became Roper's partner and fellow Prothonotary; they shared chambers at first in Lincoln's Inn, then in Crosby Place and finally in Lincoln's Inn again. Richard Heywood had another link with the More-Rastell circle. His older brother, John, married Joan the daughter of Elizabeth More and John Rastell, and sister of William Rastell. 'Merry John Heywood' was a dramatist and musician who was connected with the Court, to which he was probably introduced by Thomas More. The Heywoods were among the regular visitors to the Mores in their Chelsea days. Richard Heywood died in 1570, but John survived until 1580, when he died in exile.

Richard Heywood was present at the trial and it may safely be assumed that he would hasten to tell the family of what had taken place. The trial must also have been a subject of discussion with his partner William Roper. This evidence was supported by that of the two other named spectators, besides 'others of good credit'. Had all this been written down at once, the report would have been our primary source, but the memory of such a shattering event would not easily fade even after the passage of twenty years. Moreover, when Roper wrote down his recollections, Richard Heywood was still his partner and it would have been natural to check memories. Sir Anthony St Leger was also back in Kent at that time. We do not know anything further of John Webbe.

These facts give more authority to Roper's testimony than if he relied entirely on his recollections of what he had been able to gather from ordinary spectators. He was making use of professional observers. To this may be added that whatever official records there were, would be available to him in his official position. His narrative is of great importance, since he was the only one to give the More-Rich evidence. It has already been noted that this was lacking from the earlier accounts. The significance of this part of the trial will be discussed later; here it is pertinent to ask, Why was it omitted from the first narrative?

Professor de Vocht suggested 'that Rastell [sic] dropped the Rich incident because from a lawyer's point of view it falls short of the rest of the trial in importance.'¹ In fact, the evidence of Rich of his conversation in the Tower with More takes up a third of the indictment, and it was of primary importance in establishing the accusation that More had spoken the fatal words denying that the King could be Supreme Head. It was this that brought him within the meaning of the Act of Treason. It has also been suggested that Rastell may have had a personal motive in suppressing the Rich incident; it was 'gratitude for help or protection' from Rich while Rastell was a student at Lincoln's Inn. This is pure invention as there is simply no evidence to support it. Rich was of the Middle Temple and he would certainly not have shown favours to Sir Thomas More's nephew. Mr Derrett suggests that 'the legal arguments seemed to be the substantial part of the trial and our author [i.e. of the original account] omitted the whole episode from motives of clarity and brevity as well, perhaps, as partiality to More'. The jury must, according to this theory, have accepted Rich's version, and presumably the 'author' also agreed with this opinion. Father Bridgett suggested that 'the recital of the long dialogue, with its

---

¹ *Ordo*, p. 135. On p. 106 de Vocht states that the English original of the *Ordo* was the work of 'a well-trained and full-equipped lawyer', but William Rastell was not called to the bar until 1539.

various suppositions, and More's rehearsal of the true conversation, were probably too complicated for the French writer to follow'. Some slight support for this is found in the curious phrase used in the *News Letter* that 'eight pairs of letters' ('huict paires de lettres') passed between Fisher and More while in the Tower. This is repeated in the *Expositio* ('octo paria epistolarum') and in *Anon.* and in the German translation. Both the *Novitates* and the *Ordo* avoid this meaningless expression; the former has 'eight letters' ('actionis [octonis?] literis') and the latter 'not a few' ('litteris non paucis'). Either the writers were sticking to an alleged lost Latin original, or they were using their common sense. The Spanish translation has simply 'eight letters' ('ocho letras'). Another small pointer to a limited knowledge of English is the use of 'Gylti' in the *News Letter* for 'guilty', but this may be merely a spelling difficulty. *Novitates* and *Anon.* have the spelling 'Gylthi'. The *Expositio* surprisingly gives 'Killim'; this suggests the editor thought he knew more about English legal terms than he did. The *Ordo* rationalizes, as one may say, and gives 'they condemned the man'. Father Bridgett's suggestion is not convincing. The exchange between More and Rich was in ordinary language and was not encumbered with legal terms; it should have been the easier to follow. It must be admitted that there is no fully satisfactory solution to this problem.

II. HARPSFIELD

Nicholas Harpsfield was born in London in 1519 and after his schooling at Winchester entered New College, Oxford, in January 1535, the year of More's trial. The fate of More must have been a frequent topic of speculation at the University, where he had been a student and of which he was High Steward. Harpsfield became a Fellow in 1537. He left England in 1550, as he could not accept the changes in religion brought about by the Protector Somerset; he went to Louvain and there joined the group of voluntary exiles that included William Rastell and his wife (Winifred Clement), John Clement and his wife (Margaret Giggs), Antonio Bonvisi, the future martyr John Story, and another Fellow of New College, John Boxall, who, like Harpsfield, was to suffer many years of imprisonment under Elizabeth. The exiles remained at Louvain until the accession of Mary Tudor in July 1553. Harpsfield's close association for several years with the exiled More circle has an important bearing on the biography he was to begin a few years later. They must often have talked over their memories of happier days when Sir Thomas More was the centre round which their lives revolved. The *Expositio*, the *News Letter*, and the *Novitates* would probably be in their hands and they would discuss every detail. Not one of them, as far as is known, had been at the trial, but Margaret Clement had been in the crowd at the execution and had been at the burial. When therefore Harpsfield came to write his *Life and Death of Sir Thomas More* he had this intimate association with members of the More household as his foundation. He was, however, a rather dull man and apt to moralize, and there are signs that he did not appreciate the importance of much that he heard at Louvain. For instance, he noted that Bonvisi described talks he had had with Thomas Cromwell and the context suggests that More may sometimes have joined them. Yet Harpsfield is content to say that he had not space in his book to record what they discussed. The truth is that the liveliest parts of his book are derived from Roper. The account of the trial is based on the *News Letter* and the *Expositio* with Roper's additions. It must be accepted that the More circle regarded this conflation as a fair record as far as they could judge.

III. STAPLETON

Thomas Stapleton was born in the month and year in which Sir Thomas More was executed. Like Harpsfield, Stapleton was educated at Winchester and New College, Oxford. He left England soon after Elizabeth came to the throne (1558) and went to Louvain. We are not here concerned with his fame as a scholar and as a leading Catholic apologist. His life of More is the third part of his *Tres Thomae* (Douay, 1588), the other two being St Thomas the Apostle and St Thomas à Becket. This work was in Latin and was frequently reprinted. An English translation did not appear until 1928. So, like Harpsfield's book, Stapleton's has had to wait until this century before being made accessible to the English public.

In his Preface, Stapleton gave his sources. He had known William Rastell (d. 1565) and John Clement (d. 1572) and his wife Margaret (d. 1570) at Louvain. This was during their second period of exile; they had returned to England at the beginning of Mary's reign, but had left again in 1563. A year later John Heywood and his wife Joan Rastell joined them. Stapleton mentioned that he had also met John Heywood. Another informant was John Harris (d. 1579), who taught Greek at Louvain and later at Douai, where Stapleton moved in 1569. Harris had been More's secretary and had married Dorothy Colley, Margaret Roper's maid; she was still living at Douai in 1588 when Stapleton's book was finished. 'Nothing has helped me more', he wrote, 'than Harris's manuscript collections, including many of More's letters written in the martyr's own hand, all of which Mr Harris's widow handed over to me.' He must also have had a copy of Roper's memoir, as the Rich-More dialogue is included. There are no indications that he had seen Harpsfield's manuscript, nor does he make any reference to the book on More and Fisher that Rastell wrote during his second exile.

But for Stapleton, we should not know of a number of More's letters, but, it is sad to say, the author did not include complete copies of some and he even omitted others. 'These letters,' he wrote, referring to those not given, 'I will omit, for already my account has become longer than I expected.' Would that he had given us every word! It may also be regretted that he did not write his book in the splendid English of the translation of Bede's *Ecclesiastical History* that he made in his early days at Louvain.

It will be seen that Stapleton had good authority for what he wrote, but, apart from the letters for which his book is the only source, he did not add anything significant to what was already recorded in the manuscripts of Roper and Harpsfield. When he came to give an account of the trial he used the *News Letter* and the *Expositio* and Cardinal Pole's *De Unitate Ecclesiae*. The last did not contain a full account of the trial, but it may have been based on the lost Italian version that Pole sent to Erasmus. Dorothy Harris could not have given Stapleton any fresh information about the trial, but she was able to describe the domestic life at Chelsea and she told him a curious incident about the burial. This will be noted when we come to discuss the execution.

A biography by a young writer who concealed his name under the initials 'Ro.Ba.', written probably about 1600, remained in manuscript until it was published in 1839. The next edition was that of the Early English Text Society of 1950. It is largely a compilation from Harpsfield and Stapleton and has no independent authority, but it makes pleasant reading.

Another *Life* was begun by Father Thomas More, great-grandson of Sir Thomas, and completed by Cresacre, the youngest brother of Thomas, about 1620 and published about 1626. This added nothing to existing records apart from one or two slight family traditions. It has no importance for the trial. It was the popular biography until the appearance of Father Bridgett's biography to which reference has been made in the Preface to this book.

Chapter 3

THE SUCCESSION

I𝐓 is not proposed here to give an account of the events that led to the imprisonment of Fisher and More in the Tower. We shall have occasion to refer to some of the answers they gave in interrogations before members of the Council when we come to examine the trial in detail. It is essential, however, to have a clear understanding of three Acts of Parliament that affected them: the Succession, the Supremacy, and Treason.

On 23 May 1533 Archbishop Cranmer annulled Henry VIII's marriage with Catherine of Aragon; his marriage to Anne Boleyn was declared valid on 28 May, and on 1 June she became Queen. The Parliament called in November 1529 had been adjourned in April 1533, and its next session began in the middle of January 1534. Among its early tasks was that of legalizing the Succession, since the Princess Mary had been bastardized by the annulment of her parents' marriage. This was in some respects a unique situation. Henry VII had established himself as king, in fact, before his first Parliament met in November 1485, three months after the battle of Bosworth. A short Act was passed declaring the inheritance of the Crown to 'be, rest and remain and abide in the most royal person of our new Sovereign Lord King Henry VIIth and in the heirs of his body lawfully comen perpetually'. On 27 March

1486 Pope Innocent VIII issued a Bull recognizing Henry's title as king. The question of the Succession could have been left as it had been registered by Parliament in 1485, since the terms 'heirs of his body lawfully comen' covered the new situation, and, had Henry VIII been as wise as his father, he would have been content to avoid a closer definition, but the birth of the Princess Elizabeth in September 1533 and perhaps the importunity of her mother started him on a course that was bound to lead to trouble. Moreover, he had an itch to get his own desires approved by Act of Parliament. The first Act of Succession[1] was passed in the January-March session of 1534.[2] It has been called 'a constitutional innovation of the utmost importance. From the earliest ages the succession to the crown had in theory been determined, first by election, and then by hereditary right. In practice it had often been decided by the barbarous arbitrament of war. For right is vague, it may be disputed, and there was endless variety of opinion as to the proper claimant to the throne if Henry should die.'[3] Even so, had Henry been content with defining the line of succession, much subsequent discord would have been avoided. What emerged was, as another historian has written, 'a treatise on the canon law, a constitutional enactment, and a political manifesto'.[4] An analysis of the Act will illustrate its unique character.

Only a sixth of the text is concerned with the actual line

[1] *G & H*, pp. 232–43.

[2] A week before the prorogation Clement VII pronounced the marriage between Henry and Catherine to be valid. Seven years had passed since Henry had raised the question.

[3] A. F. Pollard, *Henry VIII*, p. 257.

[4] H. A. L. Fisher, *History of England*, 1485–1547, p. 326.

of succession. The lengthy preamble points out the troubles that had occurred in the past by the 'ambiguity and doubts' regarding the succession, though it might have been thought that the declaration of 1485 was clear enough, 'heirs of his body lawfully comen'. 'By reason of these doubts,' it was argued, 'the Bishop of Rome, and see apostolic, contrary to the great and inviolable grants of jurisdiction given by God immediately to emperors, kings and princes, in succession to their heirs, has presumed, in times past, to invest who should please them, to inherit, in other men's kingdoms and dominions, which thing we, your most humble subjects both spiritual and temporal, do most abhor and detest.' This was a travesty of the facts. It is true that the Popes claimed the right to depose princes, but by the sixteenth century this was no longer operative. The pity was that it took the Popes some time to realize this, and under Elizabeth and the early Stuarts, the Papal claim to depose princes and to free their subjects from their allegiance became a major factor in determining policy towards Catholics.

Henry VIII had not always thought in this way. Before his *Assertio Septem Sacramentorum* was published in 1521, he had asked Sir Thomas More to edit the manuscript. More thought that the King had paid too high a tribute to the authority of the Pope and he suggested that it should be 'more slenderly touched'.

> 'Nay,' quoth his Grace, 'that it shall not. We are so much bounden unto the See of Rome that we cannot too much honour it.'
> Then did I further put him in remembrance of the statute

of Praemunire whereby a good part of the Pope's pastoral cure here was passed away.

To that answered his Highness, 'Whatsoever impediment be to the contrary, we will set forth that authority to the uttermost, for we received from that See our crown imperial.'

Which, till his Grace with his own mouth told it me, I never heard before.[1]

Henry was here referring to the Bull granted his father by Innocent VIII. It will be noted that More considered the Pope's temporal power to be limited under English law; he did not, however, believe that any national law could limit the spiritual authority of the Holy See.

The Act went on to deal with the marriage between Catherine and Henry. It recited the case against the validity of the marriage. One passage should be read carefully.

. . . that the marriage heretofore solemnized between your highness and the Lady Katherine, being before lawful wife to Prince Arthur, your elder brother, which by him was carnally known, as does duly appear by sufficient proof in a lawful process had and made before Thomas, by the sufferance of God, now archbishop of Canterbury and metropolitan and primate of this realm, shall be, by authority of this present Parliament definitively, clearly, and absolutely declared, deemed and adjudged to be against the laws of Almighty God, and also accepted, reputed, and taken of no value nor effect, but utterly void and annulled, and the separation thereof, made by the said archbishop, shall be good and effectual to all intents and purposes; any licence, dispensation, or any other acts going afore, or ensuing the

[1] *Roper*, p. 68.

same, or to the contrary thereof, in any wise notwithstanding; and that every such licence, dispensation, act or acts,
thing or things heretofore had, made, done, or to be done
by the contrary thereof, shall be void and of none effect;
and that the said Lady Katherine shall from henceforth
called and reputed only dowager to Prince Arthur, and not
queen of this realm; and that the lawful matrimony had
and solemnized between your highness and your most dear
and entirely beloved wife Queen Anne, shall be established,
and taken for undoubtful, true, sincere, and perfect ever
hereafter, according to the just judgment of the said Thomas,
archbishop of Canterbury, etc.

The Act surprisingly then went on to deal with all
marriages within the prohibited degrees, a matter that had
hitherto been dealt with under canon law; it was as if
Henry was determined that no one should make the mistake that he claimed he had made. The point of this
apparently irrelevant subject lies in the words,

which marriages, although they be plainly prohibited and
detested by the laws of God, yet nevertheless at some times
they have proceeded under colours of dispensations by man's
power, which is but usurped, and of right ought not to be
granted, admitted, nor allowed; for no man of what estate,
degree, or condition soever he be, has power to dispense
with God's laws, as all the clergy of this realm in the said
Convocations, and the most part of all the famous universities of Christendom, and we also, do affirm and think.

This is the nearest approach the Act came to denying outright the competence of the Pope to grant dispensations; it
was in effect a rejection of Papal authority. It was in such

sentences that Fisher and More read the deeper significance of the Act.

Such marriages could be annulled 'by any of the archbishops, bishops, or other ministers of the Church of England', and the offspring 'shall not be lawful nor legitimate; any foreign laws, licences, dispensations, or other thing or things to the contrary thereof notwithstanding'.

At last the Act came to the determination of the Succession. After Henry's death the Crown was to go to his eldest surviving son; failing a son, it was to go to the Princess Elizabeth. Thus the Act made definite provision for 'heirs female'.

The 1st May 1534 was fixed as the date for the proclamation of the 'tenor and contents of this Act'. The rest of the Act, nearly a third of it, dealt with penalties for infringements. First of all came those guilty of high treason, defined in the Act as,

> by writing or imprinting, or by any exterior act or deed, maliciously procure or do, or cause to be procured or done, any thing or things to the peril of your most royal person, or maliciously give occasion by writing, print, deed, or act, whereby your highness might be disturbed or interrupted of the crown of this realm, or by writing, print, or act, procure or do, or cause to be procured or done, any thing or things to the prejudice, slander, disturbance, or derogation of the said lawful matrimony solemnized between your majesty and the said Queen Anne, or to the peril, slander, or disherison of any the issues and heirs of your highness, being limited by this Act to inherit or to be inheritable to the crown of this realm, in such form as is aforesaid, whereby any such issues or heirs of your highness

might be destroyed, disturbed, or interrupted in body or title of inheritance to the crown of this realm, as to them is limited in this Act in form above rehearsed; that then every such person and persons, of what estate, degree, or condition they be of, subject or resident within this realm, and their aiders, counsellors, maintainers, and abettors, and every of them, for every such offence shall be adjudged high traitors . . .

The penalty was death with forfeiture of all possessions. It will be noted that this in itself was a Treason Act.

Next came those who

after the said first day of May, by any words, without writing, or any exterior deed or act, maliciously and obstinately shall publish, divulge or utter any thing or things to the peril of your highness, or to the slander or prejudice of the said matrimony solemnized between your highness and the said Queen Anne, etc.

This was to be adjudged misprision of treason, with the penalty of 'imprisonment of their bodies at the king's will' and forfeiture of all possessions.

The Act next provided for the government of the country during a minority. This was followed by provision for the oath. The wording here is most important.

And, for the more sure establishment of the succession of your most royal majesty, according to the tenor and form of this Act, be it further enacted by authority aforesaid, that as well all the nobles of your realm spiritual and temporal, as all other your subjects now living and being, or that hereafter shall be, at their full ages, by the commandment of your majesty or of your heirs, at all times hereafter from time to time, when it shall please your highness or your heirs to appoint, shall make a corporal oath[1] in the presence of your highness or your heirs, or before such others as your majesty or your heirs will depute for the same, that they shall truly, firmly, and constantly, without fraud or guile, observe, fulfil, maintain, defend and keep, to their cunning, wit, and uttermost of their powers, *the whole effects and contents of this present Act.*

Those who 'obstinately refuse' to take the oath when commanded were guilty of misprision of high treason and liable to life imprisonment and the loss of their goods. In the first draft of the Bill, this offence was condemned as high treason but Parliament had this modified to 'misprision of high treason'.

Before Parliament was prorogued on 30 March, the members of both Houses 'most lovingly accepted and took such oath as then was devised in writing'. The wording of this oath was not given in this first Act of Succession, but the terms of the Act indicated that it covered 'the whole effects and contents'. The taking of the oath was presumably a spontaneous act, though anyone who refused (and there is no record of anyone doing so) would have become suspect. Fisher was ill at Rochester when the other bishops, as members of the House of Lords, took the oath; his summons to Lambeth on 13 April could be regarded as giving him an opportunity to follow his colleagues' example, but there was no statutory compulsion before 1 May. More was not a Member of Parliament and he was

---

[1] A corporal oath was one that was reinforced by touching a sacred object such as a copy of the Gospels.

no longer a councillor;[1] he was the only layman, as far as is known, called before the Commissioners on 13 April; he was being treated as a special case, for at Lambeth the others whose names he noted were clergy such as Rowland Phillips, Hugh Latimer and Nicholas Wilson. An oath was therefore being demanded from the clergy before 1 May.

Roper recorded that

> Whereas the oath confirming the Supremacy and Matrimony was by the first Statute in few words comprised, the Lord Chancellor and Master Secretary did of their own heads add more words unto it, to make it appear unto the King's ears more pleasant and plausible. And that oath, so amplified, caused they to be ministered to Sir Thomas More, and to all other throughout the Realm. Which Sir Thomas More perceiving, said unto my wife, 'I may tell thee, Meg, they that have committed me hither, for refusing of this oath not agreeable to the statute, are not by their own law able to justify my imprisonment. And surely, daughter, it is a great pity that any Christian Prince should by a flexible Council ready to follow his affections, and by a weak clergy lacking grace constantly to stand to their learning, with flattery be so shamefully abused.' But at length the Lord Chancellor and Master Secretary, espying their own oversight in that behalf, were fain afterwards to find the means that another Statute should be made for the confirmation of the oath so amplified with their additions.

Roper confused the question of the Supremacy and that of the Succession. The first Act of Succession made no mention of the King's assumption of the title of Supreme

---

[1] His salary was stopped at Easter 1534, a week before he was called to Lambeth.

Head, though it did, by implication, reject the authority of the Pope, since it denied him the power to grant dispensations in matrimonial cases. It also withdrew the right of appeal to Rome in such matters and at the same time transferred to Parliament the right to legislate on questions hitherto determined by canon law. Later writers, even Father Bridgett, have followed Roper here in stressing the Supremacy; it was a natural mistake, for this new title was, so to speak, the background to the new legislation, as Fisher and More were quick to recognize.

Roper's statement that Audley and Cromwell 'did of their own heads add more words unto' the oath calls for an extended comment. William Rastell also claimed that 'the oath contained more things than were warranted by the Act of Succession'.[1] It has already been noted that the oath was not included in that first Act, but on 30 March 1534 Letters Patent were issued appointing Commissioners to administer an oath; they were Cranmer, Audley, Norfolk and Suffolk.[2] The text of the oath then prescribed reads as follows:[3]

> Ye shall swear to bear your faith, truth and obedience, alonely to the King's Majesty, and to the Heirs of his body, according to the limitation and rehearsal within this Statute of Succession above specified, and not to any other within this realm, nor foreign Authority, Prince or Potentate; and in case any oath be made, or hath been made, by you to any other person or persons, that then ye to repute the same as vain and annihilate; and that, to your cunning, wit, and utter-

[1] *Harpsfield*, p. 228.
[2] See Mr Geoffrey de C. Parmiter's article 'Saint Thomas More and the Oath' in *Downside Review*, 1960.
[3] *Journals of House of Lords*, I, 82.

most your power, without guile, fraud, or other undue
means, ye shall, observe, keep, maintain, and defend, this
Act above specified, and all the whole contents and effects
thereof, and all other Acts and Statutes made since the
beginning of this present Parliament, in confirmation or
for due execution of the same, or of anything therein contained; and thus ye shall do against all manner of persons,
of what estate, dignity, degree or condition soever they be,
and in no wise do or attempt, nor to your power suffer to
be done or attempted, directly or indirectly, anything or
things, privily or apertly, to the let, hindrance, damage, or
derogation thereof, or of any part of the same, by any
manner of means, or for any manner of pretence or cause.
So help you God and all Saints.

More objected to Margaret Roper that 'the oath was
not agreeable to the statute'. What had he in mind? The
most objectionable phrase was the reference to 'any . . .
foreign Authority, Prince or Potentate', which was obviously aimed at the Pope, and did not come within the
actual wording of the Act. A further addition was the
phrase 'all other Acts or Statutes made since the beginning
of this present Parliament in confirmation or for due execution of the same'.[1] Whether, as Roper said, these additions,
or others not recorded, were made by Audley and Cromwell, is a matter of surmise. More's objection was valid,
but even had these additions not been in the oath, he would
still have had sufficient grounds for refusing to take it.

We may note here More's references to 'a flexible

[1] Mr Parmiter (*op. cit.*) rightly points out that Mgr Philip Hughes is
mistaken in applying this to all Acts of that Parliament; it applied only to
those bearing on the succession (*Reformation*, I, p. 270, n. 1).

Council' and 'a weak clergy'. One of the astonishing features of the whole matter was the ease with which both Council and clergy accepted Henry's policy. A discussion of this problem would take us too far afield, but it was an element that added to that feeling of loneliness, one might say, of desertion, that must have oppressed the two prisoners in the Tower.

When the oath was tendered to More and Fisher, each asked to see a copy of the Act; they wanted to know what were 'the whole effects and content thereof'. Both declared themselves willing to accept the line of succession laid down by Parliament but they could not accept the implications that underlay the Act. More would also note, as we have seen, the discrepancies between the oath and the Act. Cranmer suggested to Thomas Cromwell that More and Fisher should be allowed to take the oath to the succession alone, but without making this public, so that people would think they accepted the whole Act. Cromwell put this suggestion to the King, who declared that More and Fisher must take the full oath, otherwise, to quote Cromwell's letter, 'it might be taken not only as a confirmation of the Bishop of Rome's authority, but also as a reprobation of the King's second marriage'. In those words we come to the heart of the whole matter.

The Act was not only an innovation in the precision of the line of succession of named persons, but it was something new to demand an oath of 'all other your subjects'. Oaths of loyalty had always been exacted of those holding official positions or places of authority, but a general application was a new policy. It may be noted that this imposition of oaths became so much a part of Tudor legislation that the moral binding force was weakened, and those who lived into Elizabeth's reign, such as Richard Rich (d. 1567) or William Paulet (Marquis of Winchester, d. 1572) swore and forswore themselves without any qualms of conscience.

Here it may be asked, Did those who took the oath know 'the whole effects and content' of the Act? Most, of course, would accept it as something demanded by the King and therefore not to be questioned save at serious, even fatal, risk. The Act was printed by Berthelet, but its circulation would be limited and illiteracy was high. It is difficult to believe that the Commissioners appointed to tender the oath read out the Act to each person or even to a gathering of people. Most would echo the remark made by Harry Patenson (More's former jester), 'Why? What aileth him that he will not swear? Wherefore should he stick to swear? I have sworn the oath myself.'[1]

On 16 May, at seven in the morning, Eustace Chapuys, the Emperor's Ambassador, was invited to meet the Privy Council.[2] It was a formidable gathering; there were present the two Archbishops, three Bishops, the Chancellor (Audley), Thomas Cromwell (recently appointed the King's Secretary), the Duke of Norfolk (uncle of Anne Boleyn), the Marquis of Exeter (Courtenay), the Earl of Wiltshire (Anne Boleyn's father), and William Paulet, with 'the chief magistrates of this kingdom'. Why should it have been thought necessary to invite the Emperor's Ambassador to meet such an impressive assembly of councillors? The purpose was to justify the Act of Succession,

[1] *Rogers*, No 206.
[2] *S.P.(S)*, 5, i, No 58. *L.P.*, 7, i, No 690.

The Tower of London: XVIth Century

since it gravely affected the status of the Emperor's
aunt and of his cousin. The immediate purpose was clearly
put in an opening explanation by Dr Edward Foxe, the
King's Almoner and a steadfast promoter of the divorce;
he claimed that 'all and every one' of Henry's subjects had
taken the oath except 'Madame Catherine and Madame
Marie', as he called them. Had he forgotten Fisher and
More in the Tower? If the ladies were to 'persevere in their
pertinacious refusal, he [Henry] would be obliged on his
part to proceed against them according to the form and
tenor of the said statute'; this would mean a charge of
misprision of treason. Could not Chapuys, the Council
asked, persuade them to take the oath? To this he replied
by attacking the Act itself. 'The King himself,' he said,
'could not show better the invalidity of his own statute
than by compelling people to swear to it, which was a
compulsory act much condemned by the best jurists.'
Unfortunately he did not develop this idea in his despatch.
Perhaps his point was not debated. He himself was not
an expert in law, but he had facing him Bishop Tunstall,
who was an authority, having studied law at Padua
University for some years; a discussion between them
would have been enlightening. Chapuys went on, 'People
swore because they dared not offer opposition, the penalty
being forfeiture of life and property, and no one in these
times wished to become a martyr; besides which, several
reconciled themselves to the idea by the notion that oaths
taken by force, against morality, were not binding.' In
his despatch to the Emperor, Chapuys pointed out that
the lightness with which Cranmer had regarded his oath
of fidelity to the Pope when consecrated Archbishop of

Canterbury encouraged people to regard lightly any enforced oath. One would like to think that Chapuys actually said this to the Council but it is improbable that he did so. He bluntly refused to attempt to persuade Queen Catherine and the Princess Mary to take the oath, and he warned the Council that the Emperor would greatly resent the way in which his aunt had been set aside and his cousin bastardized. That, of course, was what really lay behind the conference; Henry was apprehensive as to how the Emperor would act. The argument was continued by Bishop Tunstall who, according to Chapuys, spoke without conviction; he was followed by the Bishop of London and the Archbishop of York and one or two others. They dealt mainly with the validity of the marriage with Catherine, a subject we need not go into. Cranmer and Cromwell remained silent, but the Duke of Norfolk put the politician's point of view: the marriage with Anne Boleyn was a *fait accompli* and there was no more to be said. Chapuys took the opportunity of urging that the Queen and her daughter should be treated with far more respect and consideration than they were receiving. He added that there was nothing to fear from her; she had told him on several occasions that 'no war should be made on her account'. The conference was inconclusive. The long despatch included the warning, 'It is to be feared that upon the obstinate refusal of the Queen and the Princess to comply with his wishes, the King, at the instigation of this accursed concubine of his, will play them both a bad trick.' He thought that they would be sent to the Tower.

The conference had been concerned with the effect of the Act on the positions of Queen Catherine and the

Princess Mary and not with the primacy of the Apostolic See. Fisher and More, however deeply they deplored the treatment of the Queen and her daughter, did not take the same attitude as Chapuys, who was the valiant champion, almost the only one, of his master's close relatives. Fisher and More were concerned with the more fundamental implications of the Act, since in their view it went far beyond the practical business of settling the succession to the Crown; they saw in it the first signs of a deliberate policy of separation from Rome.

More, with his intimate knowledge of the King, had early recognized the dangerous trend of his policy, or, perhaps it would be more correct to say, of his pursuit of his own passions. When in May 1533 Cranmer had pronounced the marriage with Catherine void, More said to Roper, 'God give grace, son, that these matters within a while be not confirmed with oaths.' And when the bishops urged him in vain to attend the coronation of Anne Boleyn, he had warned them that they were taking the first step on a slippery slope.

The oath set out in the Letters Patent was, with a few modifications, included in the second Act of Succession[1] passed by the Parliament that met in November 1534. The statutory oath read as follows:

> Ye shall swear to bear faith, truth, and obedience alonely to the king's majesty, and to his heirs of his body of his most dear and entirely beloved lawful wife Queen

[1] 'An Act ratifying the oath that every of the king's subjects hath taken or shall hereafter be bound to take for due observance of the Act made for the surety of the Succession of the King's Highness in the Crown of the Realm' (26 Hen. 8, c. 2).

Anne,[1] begotten and to be begotten, and further to the heirs
of our said sovereign lord according to the limitation in the
statute made for surety of his succession in the crown of
this realm, mentioned and contained, and not to any other
within this realm, nor foreign authority or potentate: and
in case any oath be made, or has been made, by you, to any
person or persons, that then ye are to repute the same as
vain and annihilate; and that, to your cunning, wit, and
uttermost of your power, without guile, fraud, or other
undue means, you shall observe, keep, maintain, and defend
the said Act of Succession, and all the whole effects and
contents thereof, and all other Acts and statutes made in
confirmation, or for execution of the same, or of anything
therein contained; and this ye shall do against all manner of
persons, of what estate, dignity, degree, or condition soever
they be, and in no wise do or attempt, nor to your power
suffer to be done or attempted, directly or indirectly, any
thing or things privily or apertly to the let, hindrance,
damage, or derogation thereof, or of any part of the same,
by any manner of means, or for any manner of pretence;
so help you God, all saints, and the holy Evangelists.

The phrases to which More objected were incorporated
in the oath. It could still be objected that they exceeded
the terms of the original Statute. It should also be noted
that the King assumed the power to absolve his subjects
from other oaths, a power previously reserved to the Pope.

This short Act further emphasized that all subjects of
the Crown were obliged to take the oath. 'The Lords
spiritual and temporal, and the Commons of this present
Parliament meant and intended that every subject of this

[1] To his daughter Margaret, More said: 'It pitieth me to remember into
what misery, poor soul, she shall shortly come' (*Roper*, p. 77).

realm should be obliged and bounden to take and accept, for maintenance and defence of the same Act, upon the pains contained in the said Act, and that every of the king's subjects, upon the said pains, shall be obliged to accept and take the said oath.' There could be no escape.

It has been said that some took the oath with reservations. William Rastell stated that his cousin, Margaret Roper, 'took the oath with this exception, as far as would stand with the law of God'. This may have been a mental reservation, but it would certainly not have been permitted as a spoken addition.

Chapter 4

THE SUPREMACY

A WHOLE volume could be written on the series of steps
by which Henry VIII, with the guidance of Thomas
Cromwell and the approval of Parliament, made himself
'Supreme Head in earth of the Church of England'. It
would not, however, add to our understanding of Sir
Thomas More's trial to retell these events in detail. It must
have been with consternation that he saw what was hap-
pening and the ease with which the King gained his will.
Fisher had raised his voice at the first encounter in Convocation in January 1531, and Cuthbert Tunstall had, at
the same time, expressed his doubts to the King himself,
but the reassurances given by Henry that he was not
claiming any spiritual authority seem to have satisfied the
Bishop.

The essential facts are set out very clearly in the following quotations.[1]

In January 1531, when parliament and the Convocations
met again after a prorogation lasting since December 1529,
a step of greater purpose was taken: the whole clergy in
their Convocations surrendered to an indictment of praemunire[2]—for exercising their spiritual jurisdiction in despite

[1] G. R. Elton, 'The Reformation in England' in *The New Cambridge
Modern History*, Vol. II (1958), pp. 233–4.
[2] A term loosely used to denote fourteenth-century Acts of Parliament

of the king's rights!—and bought a pardon for £118,000.
At the same time they acknowledged Henry as 'their only
and supreme lord and, as far as the law of Christ allows,
even supreme head'. In this surrender lay the germ of a
revolution, but for the moment Henry showed no signs of
understanding its implications. According to his own interpretation, the title gave him only temporal and no spiritual
rights of leadership.

*   *   *

Cromwell's intention was to create a self-contained and
self-sufficient realm: a sovereign national State which, using
the civilian concept of *imperium* existing in any polity whose
ruler did not recognize a superior on earth, he called the
empire of England. His own most important contribution
to the structure of this State was his understanding that this
'empire' could in England be expressed in the sovereign
legislative action of the king in parliament, embodied in
statute. Freeing statute of that older limitation which wished
to test it by reference to some external law—the law of
nature, the law of Christendom (Thomas More's test)—he
held that it was omnicompetent and must be obeyed.

The work was done in four sessions of Parliament. In
1532 Cromwell utilized some of those Commons' grievances
of 1529 to force the clergy into surrendering authority over
its laws to the Crown (the Submission of the Clergy) and
promoted a measure which deprived the pope of the

---

designed to prevent appeal from the king's courts to Rome. The original
scope was limited, but, even so, was largely inoperative except when it
suited the King and Council. The Tudor interpretation was unjustified;
the series of Acts passed under Henry VIII replaced the old ones. 'Praemunire' became a bogy-word meaning anything the King wanted it to
mean.

annates or first-fruits from England, though Henry's reluctance to go to extremes led to the inclusion of a clause which postponed the effect of the act at the king's pleasure. Thus at last the real attack on the Papacy had begun, with the undermining of its legislative and financial powers over the Church of England. In 1533 the great Act in Restraint of Appeals to Rome destroyed the most important weapon of papal interference in English affairs by prohibiting appeals from courts inside the realm to courts outside it. Its famous preamble outlined Cromwell's theory of the State by describing the empire of England. The two sessions of 1534 completed the work by transferring to the Crown all other papal powers in the Church, such as the granting of dispensations, the appointment of bishops, and the right to tax freely.

The Act of Supremacy passed in November 1534 was the culmination of a long process; it declared what, in fact, had already been achieved. The operative part is brief enough to be given in full.

Albeit the king's majesty justly and rightfully is and ought to be the supreme head of the Church of England, and so is recognized by the clergy of this realm in their Convocations, yet nevertheless for corroboration and confirmation thereof, and for the increase of virtue in Christ's religion within this realm of England, and to repress and extirp all errors, heresies, and other enormities and abuses heretofore used in the same; be it enacted by authority of this present Parliament, that the king our sovereign lord, his heirs and successors, kings of this realm, shall be taken, accepted, and reputed the only supreme head in earth of the Church of England, called *Anglicana Ecclesia*; and shall have and enjoy, annexed and united to the imperial crown of this realm, as well the title and style thereof, as all honours, dignities, pre-eminences, jurisdictions, privileges, authorities, immunities, profits, and commodities to the said dignity of supreme head of the same Church belonging and appertaining; and that our said sovereign lord, his heirs and successors, kings of this realm, shall have full power and authority from time to time to visit, repress, redress, reform, order, correct, restrain, and amend all such errors, heresies, abuses, offences, contempts, and enormities, whatsoever they be, which by any manner spiritual authority or jurisdiction ought or may lawfully be reformed, repressed, ordered, redressed, corrected, restrained, or amended, most to the pleasure of Almighty God, the increase of virtue in Christ's religion, and for the conservation of the peace, unity, and tranquillity of this realm; any usage, custom, foreign law, foreign authority, prescription, or any other thing or things to the contrary hereof notwithstanding.

The Act imposed no oath, nor were any penalties laid down; it was simply declaratory. Its comprehensive nature will be noted; there was little left to the Church of England outside the King's control both in temporal and spiritual matters for such terms as 'heresies' and 'errors' could be interpreted to cover almost anything; moreover, the King also assumed full powers of visitation and correction. Almost all the clergy, beginning with the bishops and abbots, had already accepted the new title; it will be noted that in its statutory form the qualification 'as far as the law of Christ allows' had been omitted.[1]

[1] See also, *The Tudor Constitution: Documents & Commentary*, ed. G. R. Elton (Cambridge, 1960), pp. 329–69.

It will be of interest to give the full style of the King as adopted by Parliament in 1543.

By the grace of God, King of England, France and Ireland, Defender of the Faith, and of the Church of England and also of Ireland on Earth the Supreme Head.

Chapter 5

TREASON

It has already been remarked that the Act of Succession was in effect a Treason Act, but this, wide ranging as it was, did not satisfy Henry and Cromwell. As early as January 1531 a Bill for the 'Augmentation of Treasons' had been under consideration; it was not proceeded with, perhaps because Cromwell felt that Parliament was not yet in the right mood. There are five drafts with Cromwell's annotations.[1]

Up to 1534 the law of Treason was the Act of 1352 of Edward III. The chief grounds for an accusation were compassing the king's death, levying war against him, and adhering to his enemies. Some 'overt act' was necessary to support the charge. The judges, however, had always extended the scope of the Act when it seemed justified, as the Act had been narrowly drawn. Two opinions given at the trial of Sir Nicholas Throckmorton in April 1554 may be quoted.[2] As it happened, the trial came between the repeal of Henry VIII's legislation and fresh statutes, so Throckmorton was tried under the 1352 Act. He claimed

[1] The reader will find further details in two articles: 'The Trial of Treason in England', by S. Rezneck, in *Essays in History in Honour of C. H. McIlwain* (1936), and 'Treason Legislation of Henry VIII', by I. D. Thornley, in *Trans. Royal Hist. Soc.*, 3rd Series, Vol. xi. See also *The Tudor Constitution: Documents and Commentary*, ed. G. R. Elton (Cambridge, 1960), pp. 59–63.

[2] *State Trials* (Cobbett, 1809), Vol. I, p. 870.

that the speaking of words did not constitute an offence. The Queen's Sergeant-at-law (Wm. Stanford) replied' 'You are deceived to conclude all Treasons by the statute of the 25th Edward III, for that statute is but a declaration of certain treasons which were treasons before at common law. Even so, there doth remain divers other treasons which be not expressed by that statute as the judges can declare.' The Lord Chief Justice (Sir Thomas Bromley) confirmed this by adding, 'Notwithstanding the principle, as you allege it, and the preciseness of your sticking to the bare words of the statute, it doth appear and remain of record in our learning, that divers cases have been adjudged treason without the express words of the statute.' A further opinion was given in the trial of the Duke of Norfolk in 1571,[1] when the following exchange took place.

> *Norfolk:* You say my indictment is only upon the statute of Edward III. That statute standeth upon three points, compassing the death of the Prince's person, levying of war against the Prince, and aiding the Prince's enemies, and all these must be proved by overt fact . . .
> *Catlin, L.C.J.:* Usage is the best expounder of the law, that is, the common use how the statute hath been taken and expounded, and the same statute is but the declaration of the common law.

The Act of Succession defined new treasons and others were added in later legislation. It was as if Henry, under the prompting of Cromwell, was trying to block every conceivable gap in the defences of the monarchy. Their decision to press forward with a new Treason Act may

[1] *Ibid.*, p. 958.

have been the result of the acquittal on a charge of treason in July 1534 of William, Lord Dacre of the North, Warden of the West Marches. He was tried by his peers. At this distance of time, as far as can be judged from the available evidence, it is difficult to see why he was acquitted. Treason trials were not so much legal processes as political actions, and if the King thought someone guilty of treason the chances of survival were small indeed. Yet Dacre was set free. Chapuys commented, 'This is such a novelty in England that for the past two hundred years nothing like it has been heard of, nor has a man of his class, accused of such a crime and brought to such extremity, ever escaped alive.'[1] Under the Treason Act six months later, Dacre would certainly have been condemned.

The essential part of the Act reads as follows:

> Be it therefore enacted by the assent and consent of our sovereign lord the king, and the Lords spiritual and temporal, and the Commons in this present Parliament assembled, and by the authority of the same, that if any person or persons, after the first day of February next coming, do maliciously wish, will, or desire, by words or writing, or by craft imagine, invent, practise, or attempt any bodily harm to be done to the king's most royal person, the queen's, or their heirs apparent, or to deprive them or any of them of their dignity, title, or name of their royal estates, or slanderously and maliciously publish and pronounce, by express writing or words, that the king our sovereign lord should be heretic, schismatic, tyrant, infidel or usurper of the crown, or rebelliously do detain, keep, or withhold from our said sovereign lord, his heirs or successors, any of his or their

[1] *S.P.(S)*, 5, i, No 75 (July 1534).

castles, fortresses, fortalices, or holds within this realm, etc. . . .

That then every such person and persons offending in any the premises after the said first day of February [1535], their aiders, counsellors, consenters, and abettors, being thereof lawfully convicted according to the laws and customs of this realm, shall be adjudged traitors, and that every such offence in any the premises, that shall be committed or done after the said first of February, shall be reputed, accepted, and adjudged high treason, and the offenders therein and their aiders, consenters, counsellors, and abettors, being lawfully convicted of any such offence as is aforesaid, shall have and suffer such pains of death and other penalties, as is limited and accustomed in cases of high treason.[1]

Certain phrases call for attention: 'maliciously wish, will, or desire, by words or writing', and 'maliciously publish or pronounce, by express writing or words'. Before Tudor times 'words' had been constructed as evidence of treason but usually associated with some kind of 'overt act', that is, an intention to go beyond mere words. The Commons did not like the making of 'words' alone as proof of treasonable intentions. There was a difference between accepting the ruling of judges in specific cases with all the facts before them and making 'words' as such treasonable. Moreover it opened the door wide for informers. Cromwell himself recognized that this would cause hesitation and perhaps opposition. In a note he made early in 1534 he jotted down, 'To touch the word, writing or deed. They [the Commons?] be contented that deed and writing be treason, and word be misprision with a

[1] *G & H*, 2, pp. 247–51.

declaration what the misprisions shall do.'[1] The Commons
had made the distinction in the Act of Succession between
those who actively opposed the succession and those who
refused to take the oath, but took no action. All they could
do in this new Act of Treason was to introduce the qualification 'maliciously' in two places. When he was interrogated in the Tower on 12 June 1535,[2] John Fisher said that

> When the Act by the which words were made treason
> was a-making, Robert Fisher, his brother [he was M.P. for
> Rochester], came to him to the Tower and said that there
> was an Act in hand in the Common House by which speak-
> ing of certain words against the king should be made
> treason. And because it was thought by divers of the said
> House that no man lightly could beware of the penalty of
> the said statute, therefore there was much sticking at the
> same in the Common House, and unless there were added
> in the same that the said words should be spoken maliciously,
> he thought the same should not pass.

At his trial John Fisher was to find that his claim not
to have spoken maliciously was no defence. 'To that it was
answered by some of the judges that the word maliciously
in the Statute, is but a superfluous and void word, for if a
man speak against the King's Supremacy by any manner of
means, that speaking is to be understanded and taken in
law as *maliciously*.'[3]

The meaning of the word in our common speech has
become rather restricted. The *O.E.D.* gives, with the date

[1] *L.P.*, Vol. 7, i, No 51.
[2] *L.P.*, Vol. 8, No 858. The full version, not the calendered one, is given here.
[3] *Life of Fisher* (E.E.T.S.), p. 117.

1547, the following definition, '*Law*. Wrongful intention; *esp*. that kind of evil intent which aggravates the guilt of certain offences.' But was this what the Commons meant? For lack of records, we cannot tell.

The phrase in the Act that was to prove the downfall of Fisher and More reads 'to deprive them [the King and his heirs] or any of them of their dignity, title, or name of their royal estate.'

At this point it will be helpful to remind ourselves of the chronology of these events.

1534

Parliament: Jan–March	First Act of Succession	25 Hen. VIII, cap. 22
17 April	*Fisher and More committed to Tower*	
Parliament: Nov.–Dec.	The Supremacy Act	26 Hen. VIII, cap. 1
	Second Act of Succession	26 Hen. VIII, cap. 2
	Treason Act	26 Hen. VIII, cap. 13
	Attainder of Fisher and others	26 Hen. VIII, cap. 22
	Attainder of More	26 Hen. VIII, cap. 23

The last two entries raise a question: Why were Acts of Attainder passed against Fisher and More? Under the Acts of Succession they could have been tried for misprision of treason and, if guilty, condemned to life imprisonment and forfeiture of their possessions. They could have been dealt with in the King's Bench Court. An Act of Attainder was just like any other statute; it had to be passed by the usual process through Parliament. There was no trial; there was no necessity for legal proof of guilt. It avoided awkward questions.[1]

The grounds for the Attainder of Fisher were 'contrary to the duties of allegiance, intending to sow sedition, mur-

[1] This means was last used in 1697 against Sir John Fenwick. The power still lies in Parliament, but the normal course of law is now preferred.

mur or grudge within the realm among the King's loving
and obedient subjects, by refusing the oath of succession
since 1st May'. A special clause deprived Fisher of his
bishopric,[1] a startling example of the new powers the King
now decided to exercise through Parliament over the
Church.[2] The Act against More added that he had acted
ungratefully and unkindly to the King his benefactor.

So Fisher and More were condemned to imprisonment
for life and were reduced to penury. It might have been
thought that even Henry VIII would have been satisfied
with such a severe punishment of the two men who had
withstood his will. Any fears he may have had of their
influence must have died out when he saw them deserted
by their friends; not a single bishop raised his voice in
their favour nor any member of the Council. One of
Henry's victims, John Fisher, was sixty-five years old, a
great age for that period, and he had long been enfeebled
by illness and had barely strength to walk unaided; in the
course of nature, his death was near. The other victim,
Thomas More, had retired into private life as his health,
too, was impaired; his eight months in the Tower had
weakened him and he was tortured by the stone. Yet it
was against these two ailing and helpless men that Henry
decided to go to the extreme. The tradition in the More
family was that Anne Boleyn urged that both should be
executed; alive they seemed a reproach to her. About
April 1535 it was decided to bring both if possible within

[1] In later documents he was described as 'Mr John Fisher, D.D.' In some
he is 'John Fisher, clerk', for even Henry VIII could not deprive him of his
priesthood.

[2] Presumably Parliament still has the power to deprive a bishop.

the scope of the Treason Act. Thomas More was interrogated by members of the Council on 30 April, 7 May, 3 June, and 14 June. In between the last two he had had the conversation with Rich which was to prove decisive. The purpose was to get him to speak the fatal words, 'The King cannot be Supreme Head of the Church in England.'

Chapter 6

THE INDICTMENT

ON 'Monday next after the feast of St John the Baptist', that is, on 28 June 1535, a Grand Jury at Westminster returned a true bill against Sir Thomas More, late of Chelsea. The trial was on the 'Thursday next after the morrow of St John the Baptist', that is, 1 July.

Before we discuss the trial itself it is necessary to make a study of the Indictment, a formidable document of some two thousand words.[1] It might be called 'the case for the Crown'.

The Indictment opens with a recital of the relevant parts of the Act of Supremacy and of the Act of Treason; Parliament had enacted that the King, his heirs and successors, should be accepted as the only Supreme Head in earth of the Church of England, and further that it was high treason *maliciously* to deprive the King of any part of his title in word or writing.

Then follows a detailed account of the grounds on which the Crown based the charge; this is stated at the end and reads:

> Thus the aforesaid jurors declare that the aforesaid

---

[1] The original is in the P.R.O. *Baga de Secretis*, Pouch 7, Bundle 3, m 7. The text is printed in full in *Harpsfield*, pp. 269-76. A most informative article by Mr Geoffrey de C. Parmiter on this Indictment and on the characteristics of indictments was published in the *Downside Review*, Winter, 1959-60; a shorter account is given in *Recusant History*, Vol. 6, No 3.

Thomas More, falsely, traitorously and *maliciously*, by craft imagined, invented, practised and attempted, wholly to deprive our sovereign lord the King of his dignity, title and name stated in the above mentioned statute, namely, of his dignity, title and name of Supreme Head in earth of the Church of England, to the manifest contempt of the King and in derogation of his royal crown, against the form and effect of the aforesaid statutes, and against the peace of our lord the King.

By denying, as it was claimed, the title of Supreme Head to the King, Thomas More had brought himself within the meaning of the Treason Act.

The main part of the Indictment calls for attention as it provided, one might say, the agenda for the trial. There were four counts, articles, averments or allegations.[1]

I. The first count was that on 7 May 1535, Thomas More remained obstinately and *maliciously* silent before the commissioners when asked if he accepted the King as Supreme Head. The commissioners were Thomas Cromwell, first Secretary to the King, Thomas Bedyll, clerk, Dr John Tregonwell and others of the Council. Finally he had said (the words are given in English in the Indictment), 'I will not meddle with any such matters, for I am fully determined to serve God, and to think upon His Passion and my passage out of the world.'

II. The second count stated that on 12 May, Thomas More, knowing that John Fisher was guilty of 'certain

[1] Different writers use different terms: it does not matter which is used provided it is clear to the reader that these are not four separate charges. There was one charge, that given above. I use 'count', without prejudice!

great misprisions' and that he had 'maliciously' refused to acknowledge Henry as Supreme Head, sent a number of letters by George Gold to Fisher encouraging him in his 'malicious' refusal, and telling him that he himself had kept silent. At his interrogation on that day he had said (quoted in English), 'The Act of Parliament is like a sword with two edges, for if a man answer one way, it will confound his soul, and if he answer the other way, it will confound his body.'

III. The third count is an extension of the second, but is best given separately. More, it was claimed, had feared that Fisher, at some future interrogation, might give the same answers as he himself had done, thus suggesting to the Commissioners that they were in league. Yet, when Fisher on 3 June was again examined, he refused to give a direct answer and, 'maliciously' instructed by More, declared (quoted in English), 'I will not meddle with the matter, for the statute is like a two-edged sword, and, if I should answer one way, I should offend my conscience, and, if I should answer the other way, I should put my soul in jeopardy; wherefore I will make no answer to that matter.' On the same day More was also examined and 'maliciously' refused to reply to a direct question on the Supremacy, but said (quoted in English), 'The law and statute whereby the King is made Supreme Head, as is aforesaid, is like a sword with two edges, for, if a man say that the same laws be good, then is it dangerous to the soul, and if he say contrary to the said statute, then it is death to the body. Wherefore I will make thereunto no other answer because I will not be occasion to the shortening of my life.'

The two prisoners, in order to conceal their most abominable conspiracy, then burned their letters.

On the first count More had refused to take the oath; for this he had already been attaindered. The repeated refusal could, under the Act of Treason, now be interpreted as meant 'to deprive them [the King, etc.] of their dignity, title, or name of their royal estates'.

The second and third counts alleged a conspiracy between Fisher and More; each could thus be considered among 'the aidors, counsellors, consenters and abettors' who could also be condemned for high treason.

The fourth count was intended to clinch the matter; it was evidence that More had in spoken words denied that the King could be Supreme Head. This is the most important of the allegations and one that More most strongly disputed; it must therefore be given at some length; in this part of the Indictment the conversation between More and Rich was not given in English.

IV. On 12 June, 'Richard Rich, Solicitor-General, in a conversation in the Tower with Thomas More, had in a friendly manner urged him to conform with the Acts. More replied, "Your conscience will save you; my conscience will save me." Rich, protesting that he was not speaking with authority, said, "Suppose it were enacted by Parliament that Richard Rich should be King, and that it were treason to deny it, what offence would there be if Thomas More said that Richard Rich was King? In his own conscience there could be no offence, since Thomas More was obliged to say so and accept Rich as King by the terms of the Act." More at once answered that he would commit an offence by denying Rich to be King as he was bound by an Act and was able to give his consent. This, however, he regarded as a trivial example, so he put a more serious case. "Suppose Parliament enacted that God should not be God, and that to oppose the Act would be treason, and if you, Richard Rich, were asked to say that God was not God, as required by the statute, would you commit an offence by denying it?" "Certainly," said Rich, "since it is impossible that God should not be God, but as your case is so exalted, let me put a humbler one. You know that our lord the King has been made Supreme Head in earth of the Church of England; why, therefore, Master More, should you not declare and accept him as such, just as in the first case you would accept me as King?" To this Thomas More, "maliciously" persisting in his treason, answered that "the cases are not similar, since the King can be made or unmade by Parliament; to which every subject being at the Parliament may give his consent; but, as to the supremacy, the subject cannot be bound, since he cannot give his consent in Parliament, and though the King be accepted as such in Parliament, there are many other countries that do not agree.' "

We shall have occasion to return to these statements from the Indictment when we consider how More met the several allegations.

Something should now be said of how trials for treason were then conducted. One disadvantage under which we labour is that the records of such trials during the reign of Henry VIII are scrappy, so it is impossible to compare one with another except at chance points. The unofficial reports of More's trial give us the best account we have of such a trial. For Fisher's trial we have to rely on William Rastell's account written some years afterwards; this, with some small additions, was incorporated in the earliest 'Life'[1] of Fisher written during the reign of Mary Tudor. Rastell mentioned that he had been at Fisher's execution and he may have been at the trial. There is, however, sufficient information to warrant some statements about the trials.

We must forget for the time being our present-day notions of what constitutes a fair trial. In More's time it was assumed that anyone accused of treason was guilty; there was no suggestion that the accused was innocent until proved guilty by well-sifted and tested evidence. The prisoner was not given a copy of the indictment to study beforehand, but heard it read aloud for the first time when he appeared in court. He was not allowed counsel nor could his witnesses (if they were admitted) be heard on oath. The testimony of one person was sufficient. Under Edward VI, two witnesses were required, but this was soon abrogated; there had been no such rule in previous reigns. The trial really amounted to a verbal duel between the accused and the Crown with all the advantages in favour of the prosecution. Our strict rules of evidence were unknown.

The independence of the jury had not yet been established, and, indeed, it took more than another century for that principle to become an axiom. The jury was expected to bring in a verdict in accordance with the wishes of the bench, and at times they were bullied if they dared to acquit the prisoner. Chauncy recorded that when

[1] Sometimes, but inaccurately, referred to as 'Hall's Life'. See my *Saint John Fisher*.

on 29 April the jury hesitated to bring in a verdict of
Guilty against the Carthusians, Thomas Cromwell 'by
arguments, taunts and threats' forced them to do so. There
is other evidence in support of this statement. A later incident is of interest. When Sir Nicholas Throckmorton was
tried in 1554.[1] the jury brought in a verdict of Not Guilty;
they were promptly imprisoned and not released until
they had paid heavy fines. The most significant fact,
however, is that the verdict was not reversed, and Throckmorton, no doubt to his own surprise, went free.

Trials were held in the King's Bench Court, or at sessions, but for important cases a special commission of *oyer*
and *terminer* was issued; the members of this temporary
court were not all judges or lawyers, and it gave the Crown
an opportunity for selecting commissioners of the right
colour. This packing of the bench was not regarded in those
days as scandalous; it was just part of the order of things.

The commission for the trial of Sir Thomas More on
1 July was directed to: Sir Thomas Audley (More's suc-
cessor as Lord Chancellor), the Duke of Norfolk (Anne
Boleyn's uncle), the Duke of Suffolk (the King's brother-
in-law), the Earl of Huntingdon, the Earl of Cumberland
(Lord Privy Seal), the Earl of Wiltshire (Anne Boleyn's
father), Lord Montague, Lord Rochford (brother of Anne
Boleyn), Lord Windsor, Thomas Cromwell (the King's
secretary), Sir John FitzJames (Chief Justice of the King's
Bench), Sir John Baldwin (Chief Justice of the Common
Pleas), Sir Richard Lister (Chief Baron of the Exchequer),
Sir William Paulet, Sir John Porte, Sir John Spelman, Sir
Walter Luke, Sir William Fitz-William, Sir Antony

---

[1] *State Trials* (Cobbett, 1809), Vol. I, p. 870.

FitzHerbert (Justices); nineteen in all, thirteen of whom had presided over the trial of John Fisher a fortnight earlier.

The trial took place in Westminster Hall and More was brought to the King's Bench Court. The visitor to the Hall today will need to use his imagination to re-create the scene. He must dismiss from his mind the dramatic spectacles presented by the later trials of Strafford, Charles I, and Warren Hastings. At the south end of the Hall, where the broad flight of steps now leads up to the door to St Stephen's, there were two courts, one on either side of the present doorway. There was no door at that period. On the left was the King's Bench Court and, on the right, the Chancery. The frontispiece to this volume shows these courts in the late sixteenth century. This is the earliest known picture of the interior of the Hall. Each court was about twenty-five feet in breadth. It is difficult to see how all those concerned in the trial could be squeezed into such a small space. The jury was perhaps in the lower of the galleries or boxes on the left. To complete the scene it should be remembered that the floor of the Hall was used as a meeting-place for lawyers and their clients and was open to the public and to stray dogs! Even in those days there were stalls for the sale of lawyer's stationery and other goods. It is doubtful if anyone on the floor could have heard much of what went on in the courts. Where, in this busy scene, can we picture the observer who sent his report to Paris? The upper gallery may have been open to relatives and friends and privileged persons. We know that none of the More family was there; this may have been at the wish of Sir Thomas himself, but it seems more likely that it was at the King's order that they absented themselves.

Chapter 7

THE TRIAL: FIRST COUNT

NICHOLAS HARPSFIELD's narrative is taken as the basis for the following study of the trial. Passages from his book are printed in italics;[1] illustrative and explanatory material is drawn from several sources such as More's correspondence and writings and the official reports of interrogations. We should remind ourselves that the account of the trial that has come down to us is far from being a full record; it lacks, for instance, arguments that must have been put forward by the Attorney-General. When we consider how fragmentary are the reports of other trials, apart from Fisher's, we must be grateful for what we have.

One general remark may be made. However interesting the trial may be from a legal or constitutional aspect, important as these are, it was not for More a purely legal battle. As an experienced and learned lawyer, he naturally seized on any legal point that could be argued, but such matters were of subsidiary interest to him. The overwhelming consideration for him was his conviction that religious principles must come first, and that situations could arise when the individual had to make his choice between obeying the law of God as revealed in conscience and submitting to man-made law. It was a conflict between the law of Christ as represented by the Catholic Church,

[1] The spelling has been modernized.

and the law of Parliament. Here each man had to determine his own course of conduct. More never criticized the members of his family or his friends for taking the oath; nor did he attempt to persuade them to make the decision he felt compelled to make. He put his position clearly before the commissioners at Lambeth on 13 April 1534.

> In my conscience this was one of the cases in which I was bounden that I should not obey my prince, since that whatsoever other folk thought in the matter (whose conscience and learning I would not condemn nor take upon me to judge), yet in my conscience the truth seemed on the other side. Wherein I had not informed my conscience neither suddenly nor slightly but by long leisure and diligent search of the matter.[1]

★   ★   ★

> *Sir Thomas More being brought to Westminster Hall to his arraignment at the King's Bench before fifteen Commissioners appointed for that purpose, after that his Indictment was read, as well as the Lord Chancellor as the Duke of Norfolk said to him, 'Sir Thomas More, ye see that ye have heinously offended the King's Majesty, howbeit we are in very good hope (such is his great bounty, benignity and clemency) that if you will forethink and repent yourself, if you will revoke and reform your wilful, obstinate opinion that you have so wrongfully maintained and so long dwelt in, that ye shall taste of his gracious pardon.'*

Harpsfield's 'fifteen commissioners' does not agree with the nineteen mentioned in the warrant; perhaps four were absent. As it is worded the passage suggests a kind of duet by Audley and Norfolk,[2] but each may have spoken

---

[1] *Rogers*, No 200.
[2] *Novitates* and the *Ordo* give the words to Norfolk alone.

separately and the words are a conflation of what they said.
As Lord Chancellor, Audley would preside and open the
court; his offer of pardon may have been confirmed by
Norfolk who was Lord Treasurer and the leading peer in
the Council. It is difficult to feel any respect for either man.
Audley had succeeded More as Chancellor of the Duchy
of Lancaster, as Speaker of the Commons, and finally as
Lord Chancellor. He was not a man of outstanding
ability, but he was willing to be a tool in the hands of the
King. In August 1534 More's stepdaughter, Lady Alington,
met Audley during a stay in Suffolk and she took the chance
to beg him to show favour to Sir Thomas. Audley
laughingly told her two fables; neither was closely appo-
site, but their moral seemed to be that wise men conform
to popular opinion and adjust their consciences accordingly. Norfolk was never far from the seat of government,
but he lacked the qualities of a statesman. He was an efficient soldier and could carry out instructions, but he could
not originate policy; his ambition led him to intrigue
against Wolsey and later against Cromwell. He was one
of the judges at the trial of the Carthusians and others
and he went to Tyburn to watch their last agony; he was
also one of Fisher's judges; in later years he ruthlessly
suppressed the Pilgrimage of Grace; he was one of
the judges of his niece, Anne Boleyn, in 1536 and
six years later of his other niece Catherine Howard,
and in 1546 he watched the burning of Anne Askew.
He became a harbinger of death to his relatives and
colleagues. But for the timely death of Henry VIII, in
1547, Norfolk himself would have gone to the block.
'Hot-tempered, self-seeking and brutal' is the historian's

Westminster Hall

St. Stephen's Chapel

Westminster: XVIth Century

summing-up.[1] There was a period when he was on friendly terms with Sir Thomas More, but we need not suppose that the long-faced, thin-lipped man of Holbein's portrait had any compunction when he saw the former Lord Chancellor enter Westminster Hall. It may be that when, twelve years later, Norfolk himself was expecting to be summoned to the scaffold, he recalled the conversation he once had with More.

> As the Duke of Norfolk and Sir Thomas More chanced to fall in familiar talk together, the Duke said unto him, 'By the Mass, Master More, it is perilous striving with princes. And therefore I would wish you somewhat to incline to the King's pleasure, for, by God's body, Master More, *Indignatio principis mors est.*' 'Is that all, my lord?' quoth he. 'Then in good faith there is no difference between your grace and me, but that I shall die today, and you tomorrow.'[2]

It is doubtful if any of the commissioners felt much compassion for More, though they may have felt uneasy at being the judges of such a man; some may have thought that he had suffered enough. They had all taken the oath, so why shouldn't he do the same? Moreover it was a hard age, as we should think, and disgrace and execution were the accepted hazards of public life.

The offer of pardon made at the opening of the trial may be regarded as a normal proceeding. Had More at once declared that he would accept Henry as Supreme Head, he would not have gone free; he would have

[1] Mandell Creighton (*D.N.B.*).
[2] *Roper*, p. 71.

been sent back to the Tower to remain a life prisoner.

'My Lords,' quoth Sir Thomas More, 'I do most humbly thank your Honours of your great good will towards me. Howbeit, I make this my boon and petition unto God as heartily as I may, that He will vouchsafe this my good, honest and upright mind to nourish, maintain and uphold in me even to the last hour and extreme moment that ever I shall live. Concerning now the matters you charge and challenge me withal, the articles are so prolix and long that I fear, what with my long imprisonment, what for my long lingering disease, what for my present weakness and debility, that neither my wit, nor my memory, nor yet my voice, will serve to make so full, so effectual and sufficient answer as the weight and importance of these matters doth crave.'

When he had thus spoken, sustaining his weak and feeble body with a staff he had in his hand, commandment was given to bring him a chair, wherein, being set, he commenced his answer much after this sort and fashion:

More's plea that his debility made it difficult for him to deal adequately with the Indictment was based on fact. He had been in the Tower for fifteen months and his health had deteriorated. On 14 June 1532 he had written to Erasmus[1], 'For some sort of chest complaint has laid hold of me . . . after being troubled with this ailment continually for several months, I consulted the doctors, who said that such a lingering disease could be dangerous; in their opinion no speedy cure was possible.' After More had been in prison for five months, Margaret Roper wrote to Alice Alington, ' when I had a while talked to him, first of his diseases, both in his breast of old, and his reigns now by reason of gravel and stone, and of cramp also that divers

[1] *Allen,* No 2659.

nights grippeth him in his legs . . .' When Lady Alice More appealed to the King at the end of 1534 she wrote of her husband's 'great continual sickness of body'.[1]

The injustice of withholding a copy of the Indictment from a prisoner before and during his trial stands out more clearly when he was in reduced physical condition through long months of confinement. More did not complain of that, as he knew it was the established practice, but standing for some hours would have reduced his powers of resistance. There was no sign of any decline in his mental alertness; what he feared was physical collapse. A chair was brought for him as a concession. 'Sustaining his weak and feeble body with a staff' is not given in the *News Letter*, nor in *Novitates* nor the *Ordo*. Harpsfield must have got it from the *Expositio*, where, however, its application is not quite clear. 'The prisoner made the long journey supported by a staff, his body weakened by serious illness in prison, but there was no sign of distress on his countenance.' Certainly if the writer meant that the whole of the two-and-a-half miles journey from the Tower was made on foot, More must have been exhausted by the time he reached Westminster. The meaning is not certain; it may refer to the distance down the Hall to the court. Fisher had been brought 'part by horseback and part by water' to his trial. This may have been an imaginative touch added by the writer of the *Expositio*.

'*Touching the first article, wherein it is purposed that I, to utter and shew my malice against the King and his late marriage, have ever repined*[2] *and resisted the same, I can say nothing but*

---

[1] *Rogers*, Nos 206 and 212.
[2] Murmured against.

this; that of malice I never spake anything against it, and that whatsoever I have spoken in that matter, I have none otherwise spoken but according to my very mind, opinion and conscience. In the which if I had not, for discharging of my conscience to God and my duty to my Prince, done as I have done, I might well account myself a naughty, unfaithful and disloyal subject. And for this mine error (if I may call it an error, or if I have been deceived therein) I have not gone scot free and untouched, my goods and chattels being confiscate, and myself to perpetual prison adjudged, where I have now been shut up about fifteen months.'

This first part of More's defence presents a problem. He spoke of 'the King and his late marriage', but there is no reference to this subject in the Indictment. It was there stated that on 7 May 1535 he had refused to give a direct answer when he was asked if he accepted the King as Supreme Head. It is difficult to believe that at the beginning of his trial, while his mind was fresh, More, the trained lawyer, should have misunderstood the first count against him, unless he was deliberately going back to the origin of his troubles. There is the possibility that the observer got things out of order. He was probably unable to take notes on the spot and had to rely on his memory when he came to write his report; how long afterwards this was we do not know. It is usually assumed that he at once wrote a despatch that was then taken to Paris, but it is just as likely, as has already been suggested, that he himself went to Paris and then wrote his account of the trial. This might mean an interval of ten days or a fortnight. All in the court must have been aware that the King's marriage was the beginning of the business before them, yet More, having refused to take the oath to the Succession, had already been attaindered, as he here reminded the court, on that ground. The trial had shifted from the Succession to the denial of the title of the Supreme Head.

As the marriage question was the true background of the trial, it is as well to remind ourselves of More's dealings with the problem. He wrote an account to Cromwell in a letter dated 5 March 1534 from Chelsea.[1] The King had first expressed his doubts about the marriage to More after he had returned with Wolsey's flamboyant embassy to Calais towards the end of September 1527. The King

> showed me that it was now perceived, that his marriage was not only against the positive laws of the Church and the written law of God, but also in such wise against the law of nature. Now so was it that before my going over the sea, I had heard certain things moved against the bull of dispensation concerning the Law Levitical and the Law Deuteronomical[2] to prove the prohibition to be *de iure divino*, but yet perceived I not at that time but that the greater hope of the matter stood in certain faults that were founden in the bull, whereby the bull should by the law not be sufficient.

The King then opened a Bible and pointed out the texts,

> and asked me further what myself thought thereon. At which time not presuming to look that his Highness should anything take that point for the more proved or unproved for my poor mind in so great a matter, I showed nevertheless as my duty was at his commandment what thing I thought

[1] *Rogers*, No 199.
[2] Lev. xx, 21; Deut. xxv, 5; the second is at variance with the first, but Henry took his choice.

upon the words which I there read. Whereupon his Highness accepting benignly my sudden unadvised answer commanded me to commune further with Master Foxe, now his Grace's Almoner, and to read a book[1] with him that was in making for that matter.

There the matter rested for the time being. When two years later the Legatine Court sat to decide the issue

I never meddled therein, nor was a man meet to do, for the matter was in hand by an ordinary process of the spiritual law, whereof I could little skill.

Meanwhile in 1529 More had gone with Tunstall on the embassy that brought the Peace of Cambrai. The legatine court was held at Blackfriars while they were away.

After my coming home his Highness of his only goodness (as far unworthy as I was thereto) made me, as you well know, his Chancellor of this realm, soon after which time his Grace moved me again eftsoons, to look and consider his great matter, and well and indifferently to ponder such things as I should find therein. And if it so were that thereupon it should hap me to see such things as should persuade me to that part, he would gladly use me among other of his councillors in that matter, and nevertheless he graciously declared unto me that he would in no wise that I should other thing do or say therein, than upon that that I should perceive mine own conscience would serve me, and that I should first look unto God and after God unto him, which

[1] This could not have been the collection of University opinions published in 1531, as *Rogers*, p. 494n suggests; the University campaign did not begin until the autumn 1529. The word 'book' did not always mean a printed book; Foxe and others may have drawn up a statement of the case.

most gracious words was the first lesson also that ever his Grace gave me at my first coming into his noble service.

The King once more asked More to consult with those who were fully informed of the matter, but, in spite of a careful study of the problem, More still found himself unable to conform to the King's wish.

His Highness graciously taking in good part my good mind in that behalf used of his blessed disposition in the prosecuting of his great matter only those whose conscience his Grace perceived well and fully persuaded upon that part, and as well myself as any other to whom his Highness thought the thing to seem otherwise, he used in his other business, abiding nevertheless gracious lord unto any man, nor never was willing to put any man in ruffle or trouble of his conscience. After this did I never nothing more therein, nor never any word I wrote I therein to the impairing of his Grace's part neither before nor after, nor any man else by my procurement, but settling my mind in quiet to serve his Grace in other things, I would not so much as look nor wittingly let lie by me any book of the other part, albeit that I gladly read afterward divers books that were made on his part.

More claimed that his inability to see eye-to-eye with the King on 'his great matter' was not through obstinacy or factious opposition. His conduct bore this out. He took no part in the discussions; he made no attempt to recruit supporters for his view; he remained quiet. The King was content to accept this position until his affairs reached a crisis; the interminable negotiations with Rome and the procrastination of the Pope and his own torturing desire for Anne Boleyn and her importunities finally drove him to regard as enemies all who did not actively support him. More perhaps never realized how significant his self-imposed silence seemed to others; those who had doubts must have interpreted his silence as unspoken dissent. The King and Cromwell were aware of this; they wanted spoken assent, not only to the annulment of the marriage pronounced by Archbishop Cranmer but to the further pronouncement by the clergy and by Parliamentary statute that Henry was Supreme Head of the English Church. It was not possible to separate the two issues except on paper, and it may be that More thought it best to make his position quite clear on this subject at the beginning of his defence, though as the report stands it looks like a departure from the actual substance of the Indictment, turning as it did on the Supremacy.

> '*Whereas now farther to this article is contained that I have incurred the danger and penalty of the last Act of Parliament made since I was imprisoned, touching the King's Supremacy, and that I have as a rebel and traitor gone about to rob and spoil the King of his due title and honour, and namely for that I am challenged for that I would not answer Master Secretary and others of the King's Privy Council, nor utter my mind unto them, being demanded what I thought upon the said Statute, either in liking or disliking, but this only, that I was a man dead and mortified toward the world, and to the thinking upon any other matters than upon the Passion of Christ and passing out of the world; touching, I say, this challenge and accusation, I answer that, for this my taciturnity and silence, neither your law nor any law in the world is able justly and rightly to punish me, unless you may besides lay to my charge either some word or some fact in deed.*'

More here turned directly to the terms of the Indictment. The date, 7 May, must first be examined. In the presence of Thomas Cromwell, Thomas Bedyll, John Tregonwell and others, More, it was claimed, maliciously and obstinately remained silent when asked if he accepted the King as Supreme Head, and added (the words were given in English in the Indictment), 'I will not meddle with any such matters, for I am fully determined to serve God and to think upon His Passion and my passage out of this world.' More wrote his own account of his first interrogation to Margaret Roper.[1]

> Coming into the chamber where his Mastership [Cromwell] sat with Mr Attorney, Mr Solicitor, Mr Bedyll and Mr Doctor Tregonwell, I was offered to sit with them, which I in no wise would. . . . Then his Mastership declared unto me that since it was now by Act of Parliament ordained this his Highness and his heirs be, and ever right have been, and perpetually should be, Supreme Head in earth of the Church of England under Christ, the King's pleasure was that those of his Council there assembled should demand mine opinion and what my mind was therein.

It may be noted that Cromwell used the words 'under Christ'; these were not in the Act which had omitted a somewhat similar qualification made by the clergy when the matter was first raised in Convocation. Was this a deliberate attempt to deceive More or was it a slip of the tongue?

> Whereunto I answered that in good faith I had well trusted that the King's Highness would never have commanded

[1] *Rogers*, No 214.

any such question to be demanded of me, considering that I ever from the beginning well and truly from time to time declared my mind unto his Highness, and since that time I had I said unto your Mastership Master Secretary also, both by mouth and by writing. And now I have in good faith discharged my mind of all such matters and neither will dispute the King's titles nor Pope's, but the King's faithful subject I am and will be, and daily I pray for him and for all his and for you all that are of his honourable Council, and for all the realm, and otherwise than this I never intend to meddle.

Whereunto Master Secretary answered that he thought this manner answer should not satisfy nor content the King's Highness, but that his Grace would exact a more full answer. . . .

Whereunto I shortly (after the inward affection of my mind) answered for a very truth, that I would never meddle in the world again, to have the world given me. And to the remnant of the matter, I answered in effect as before, shewing that I had fully determined with myself, neither to study nor meddle with any matter of this world, but that my whole study should be upon the Passion of Christ and mine own passage out of this world.

It will be noted that Cromwell, Bedyll and Tregonwell are also mentioned in the Indictment. The Attorney-General was Sir Christopher Hales; the Solicitor-General was Richard Rich. This surely refers to the same interrogation as that in the Indictment, yet More states that it took place 'on Friday the last day of April in the afternoon'. There is no reference in his letters to an interrogation on 7 May, nor is there any record in the State Papers. It is hardly likely that More made a mistake, since he was writing only a few days later. It is difficult to see why the date was put on a week in the official version. The Treason Act had come into force on 1 February, not 1 May, and the Act of Supremacy was declaratory without any specified date. As far as is known, More did not challenge the date, though this could have affected the validity of the Indictment. What he did challenge was the alleged intention of his silence.

At this point the Attorney-General, Sir Christopher Hales, interrupted him.

> *To this the King's Attorney occurring,*[1] *'Marry,' quoth he, 'this very silence is a sure token and demonstration of a corrupt and perverse nature, maligning and repining against the Statute; yea, there is no true and faithful subject that being required of his mind and opinion touching the said Statute that is not deeply and utterly bound, without any dissimulation, to confess the Statute to be good, just and lawful.'*
>
> *'Truly,' quoth Sir Thomas More, 'if the rule and maxim of the civil law*[2] *be good, allowable and sufficient, that Qui tacet, consentire videtur (he that holdeth his peace seemeth to consent), this my silence implieth and importeth rather a ratification and confirmation than any condemnation of your Statute. For as for that you said, that every good subject is obliged to answer and confess, ye must understand that, in things touching conscience, every true and good subject is more bound to have respect to his said conscience and to his soul than to any other thing in all the world besides, namely, when his conscience is in such a sort as mine is, that is to say, where the person giveth no occasion of slander, of tumult and sedition against his Prince, as it is with me;*

[1] Opposing.
[2] The *News Letter* has 'le droict commun'; the *Expositio*, 'legibus'; *Novitates*, 'ius commune'; the German version, 'in weltlichen Rechten'.

*for I assure you that I have not hitherto to this hour disclosed and
opened my conscience and mind to any person living in all the
world.'*

The argument may have been truncated in the report.
More was certainly not asking that his silence should be
interpreted as his assent. The Attorney claimed that the
law required positive acceptance and that refusal to speak
implied disloyalty. More's point seems to have been that
as the Act contained no specific declaration that silence
meant refusal, his silence could not be construed as such
under common law. More went on to deal with two
points of crucial importance: the clash between the conscience of the individual and the State, and his own ab-
stention from any kind of proselytism.

The first consideration goes to the heart of the whole
matter and presents what is a perennial problem. The text,
the first part of which is beloved of dictators, 'Render
therefore unto Caesar the things which are Caesar's; and
unto God the things that are God's', poses the problem.
The Church has always taught that there need be no clash
between the two duties provided the demands of the civil
authorities do not usurp the duties of men to God. The
practical, and sometimes soul-searching problem is where
to set the bounds of civil obedience; this can only be solved
by the individual himself when he is faced with the
dilemma. More put the matter quite clearly when he told
his judges that 'every true and good subject is more bound
to have respect to his said conscience than to any other
thing in all the world besides'. He was indeed making his
fundamental objection to the Act of Supremacy; it was an

invasion of that liberty of conscience that is part of the Divine Law. One of More's predecessors as Chancellor, Bishop Robert Stillington, had declared in 1468 that 'justice was ground, well and root of prosperity, peace and public rule of every realm, whereupon all the laws of the world had been grounded and set, which resteth in three: that is to say, the law of God, the law of Nature, and positive law'. That had always been the teaching of the Church. Serjeants-at-law had to swear to give counsel according to the law, 'that is to say, the Law of God, the law of reason, and the law of the land'. Statute law under Henry VIII began to invade the territory ruled by the law of God, since it subjected the conscience of the individual to the direction of the State. In this light we can see More's case as a protest against the increasing powers taken by King and Parliament to rule men's consciences.

English law now recognizes the conscientious objector, but no such position was allowed under Tudor legislation. In his *Utopia* More had permitted religious nonconformity in that Non-Christian Commonwealth.

> It should be lawful for every man to favour and follow what religion he would, and that he might do the best he could to bring others to his opinion, so that he did it peaceably, gently, and soberly without haste and contentious rebuking and inveighing others. . . . To him that would vehemently and fervently in this cause strife and contention, was decreed banishment and bondage.

More made two claims: that he had given 'no occasion of slander, of tumult and sedition against his Prince', and that he had, in fact, not even discussed his 'conscientious objection' with anyone. There is plenty of evidence that he had consistently followed this policy. When the commissioners at Lambeth tendered him the oath of 13 April 1534, he said,

> How best (so help me God), as touching the whole oath, I never withdrew any man from it, nor never advised any to refuse it, nor never put, nor will, any scruple in any man's head, but leave every man to his own conscience. And me thinketh in good faith, that so were it good reason that every man should leave me to mine.[1]

Not even Margaret, his daughter, was aware of his true reasons for refusing to take the oath and to accept the Supremacy. In his early days in the Tower he wrote to her:

> Wherein as touching the points of your letter, I can make none answer, for I doubt not but you will remember, that the matters which move my conscience (without declaration whereof I can nothing touch the points) I have sundry times shewed you that I will declare them to no man.[2]

The same attitude is taken in two letters written at later dates in the Tower. The first was to a fellow prisoner, Dr Nicholas Wilson, an old friend with whom he had studied the marriage problem. Wilson had refused the oath, but began to have doubts during his imprisonment, so he wrote to More asking for guidance. In a long and interesting reply, More said:

> As touching the oath, the causes for which I refused it, no

[1] *Rogers*, No 200.
[2] *Rogers*, No 202.

man knoweth what they be, for they be secret in mine own conscience, some other peradventure, than those that other men would think, and such as I never disclosed unto any man yet nor never intend to do while I live.[1]

Wilson had to make his own decision; More would not make it for him.

The second letter, dated 16 January 1534, was to a priest named Leder of whom nothing further is known. He seems to have heard a rumour that More had taken the oath and asked for information.

> But I thank our Lord [replied More], that the thing that I do is not for obstinacy but for the salvation of my soul, because I cannot induce mine own mind otherwise to think than I do concerning the oath. As for other men's consciences, I will be no judge of, nor I never advised any man neither to swear nor to refuse.[2]

Of all his friends Cuthbert Tunstall (Bishop of Durham from 1530) would have been the one in whom More might have confided. During their embassy to Cambrai in 1529 they must have discussed the marriage proceedings then beginning at Blackfriars, though at that time the question of the Supremacy had not been raised. When this did come up, Tunstall was in the north, where Henry kept him as much as possible, so the two friends may not have had an opportunity for private talk. The Bishop wrote to the King asking for reassurances that the Supremacy was in temporal and not in spiritual matters. Henry replied at some length, but evaded the direct issue. Tunstall,

[1] *Rogers*, No 208.
[2] *Rogers*, No 213.

however, was satisfied and joined with the York Convocation in accepting the Supremacy. It seems that More had some hope that his friend might refuse to accept the new title. Tunstall sent one of his servants to see More and Fisher in the Tower. More asked if there was any likelihood of Tunstall joining them; the servant replied that he did not know his master's mind. 'If he do not, no force,'[1] said More, 'for if he live he may do more good than die with us.'[2]

More had deliberately cut himself off from the support and comfort that can come from the understanding of friends, and his increasing loneliness is a marked characteristic of his last months. He could quite justly argue that his scrupulous conduct was in itself evidence that he was not guilty of 'slander, of tumult and sedition against his Prince', and he rightly claimed that the court must prove 'either some word or some fact in deed' to establish the charge of treason. Least of all could it be said that there was any malicious intention in his conduct.

[1] No matter.
[2] Tunstall was imprisoned in the Tower during the reign of Edward VI and deprived; Mary restored him, but he was again deprived under Elizabeth and died at the age of eighty-five at Lambeth, where he was buried. Christopher Chaytor, Tunstall's Registrar, recorded this incident in 1539.

Chapter 8

THE TRIAL: SECOND AND THIRD COUNTS

It will be simpler to take the second and third counts together, as one leads to the other.

The second Article did enforce also the foresaid accusation of transgressing the foresaid last Statute touching the King's Supremacy; for that Sir Thomas More (as it was pretended) wrote divers letters to the Bishop of Rochester, willing him in no wise to agree and condescend to the said Statute. 'Would God,' quoth Sir Thomas More, 'that these letters were now produced and openly read; but forasmuch as the said Bishop, as ye say, hath burned them, I will not stick truly to utter myself, as shortly as I may, the very tenor of the same. In one of them there was nothing in the world contained but certain familiar talk and recommendations, such as was seemly and agreeable to our long and old acquaintance. In the other was contained my answer that I made to the said Bishop, demanding of me what thing I answered at my first examination in the Tower upon the said Statute. Whereunto I answered nothing else but that I had informed and settled my conscience, and that he should inform and settle his. And other answer, upon the charge of my soul, made I none. These are the tenors of my letters, upon which ye can take no hold or handfast by your law to condemn me to death.'

After this answered he to the third article, wherein was laid to his charge that, as such time as he was examined in the Tower, he should answer that the Statute was like a two-edged sword, the which if any man would keep and observe, he should thereby lose his soul, and in case any man did not observe it, he should lose his corporal life. 'The very same answer,' said they, 'the Bishop of Rochester made, whereby it doth evidently appear that it was a purposed and a set matter between you, by mutual conference and agreement.'

To this Sir Thomas More answered that he did not precisely, but conditionally, answer, that in case the Statute were like to be a double-edged sword, he could not tell in the world how a man should demean and order himself but that he should fall into one of the dangers. 'Neither do I know what kind of answer the Bishop of Rochester made; whose answer, if it were agreeable and correspondent to mine, that hap happed[1] by reason of the correspondence and conformity of our wits, learning and study, not that any such thing was purposely concluded upon and accorded betwixt us. Neither hath there at any time any word or deed maliciously escaped or proceeded from me against your Statute, albeit it may well be that my words might be wrongfully and maliciously reported to the King's Majesty.'

It has already been noted that the references in the early narratives to the letters that passed between Fisher and More are puzzling: 'huict paires de letters', 'octo paria epistolarum'. The observer had probably misunderstood what was said at the trial; the number eight may have been mentioned, though the Indictment does not give any number. The point, however, has no significance.

Fortunately the exchange of letters between the prisoners had been the subject of five interrogations in the Tower. George Gold, servant to the Lieutenant of the Tower, was questioned on 8 June; John à Wood, More's

[1] Chance happened.

servant on the 10th, and Richard Wilson, Fisher's servant on the following day. John Fisher himself was questioned on 12 June and Thomas More on the 14th. It was evident that the Council was determined to ferret out any treasonous correspondence.

More had been able to get letters to his daughter Margaret and had corresponded with Dr Nicholas Wilson and with the priest Leder, and there is one letter to Antonio Bonvisi. There were probably others that are not extant. John à Wood may have smuggled out some letters, but George Gold, who was illiterate, seems to have been the messenger within the Tower and at least one letter to Margaret was entrusted to him.

The examiners, except for the Lieutenant, Sir Edmund Walsingham, were Cromwell's men; two, Dr Robert Aldridge and Dr Hugh Curwen, had been active in support of the King's proceedings; John Whalley had been put in charge of the London Charterhouse; Dr Thomas Leigh, Dr Richard Layton, and John ap Rice were to be visitors to the monasteries; Thomas Bedyll, Clerk to the Council, we have already met. Layton and Bedyll were priests.

The first to be questioned was George Gold. His statements were as follows:

> Says that on Sunday last, Master Fisher wrote a letter to Master More and sent it by him. The next day More sent back an answer, with Fisher's letter. Burned both at Fisher's order.
>
> About ten days ago, Fisher sent a letter to More by him and More caused him to burn it. The next day More wrote an answer and sent it by him. Fisher told him to burn it.

Has conveyed about a dozen letters between More and Fisher.

Does not know of Fisher sending letters, except to More.

John à Wood's interrogation came next. Roper recorded that when More first entered the Tower

he called unto him one John à Wood, his own servant, there appointed to attend upon him, who could neither write nor read, and sware him before the Lieutenant that if he should hear or see him, at any time, speak or write any manner of thing against the King, the Council, or the state of the Realm, he should open it to the Lieutenant, that the Lieutenant might incontinent reveal it to the Council.

As we shall see, More's letters and notes were not of this character. There is another reference to Wood in one of Margaret Roper's letters to her father she desired 'above all worldly things to be in John Wood's stead to do you some service'.

His testimony on 10 June was that

about a fortnight after the first being of the Council in the Tower, George, the Lieutenant's servant, came to More and asked him from Fisher what answer he had made. More replied that he would not dispute of the King's title, but give himself to his beads and think on his passage hence; and thus he wrote in a letter to be given to Fisher. Soon after he sent another letter by George to the effect he would not counsel Fisher to make the same answer, lest the Council might think they were agreed, and that he would not meddle with no man's conscience but his own. After the Council were at the Tower, Fisher sent to tell More what answer he had made. Does not know if More sent an answer.

The interrogation of Richard Wilson took place on the following day. William Rastell declared that 'Wilson, like a false knave, accused his master to Cromwell'. He was, in fact, the third of the servants to be questioned and, unless they were kept apart, Wilson probably knew what the other two had said; he had no startling revelations to make. The examiners suspected that it was Sir Thomas More who had drawn Fisher's attention to the word 'maliciously' in the Act, but Wilson declared that it was Robert Fisher who had discussed this with his brother.[1]

When asked if he suspected that Fisher and More were in correspondence, Wilson said he had

> heard my lord [Fisher] tell George Gold that there was no peril in the statutes except it were maliciously done or spoken, and suspects he bade George tell More so about seven or eight days before the last coming of the Council [11 June]. Heard from George that Master More said Master Secretary gave him very good words but he would say nothing about his answer.

When asked if he had taken anything to More or his servant, Wilson replies he had

> never sent anything concerning the King's matter, either in word or writing. Sent to Master More's servant half a custard on Sunday last, and long since greensauce [salad]. More or his servant sent him an image [picture] of St John, and apples and oranges after the snow that fell in winter. On New Year's Day, More sent him a paper with writing, £2000 in gold, and an image of the Epiphany.

[1] In the Latin version of the early biography of Fisher it is stated that, after his master's execution, Wilson went to the Low Countries and became a priest.

The '£2,000 in gold' was probably a little jest, perhaps a drawing of a bag of gold, or a play on George Gold's name. Wilson further stated that he had 'often suspected George Gold of carrying letters between my lord and Master More', and 'he gave George a letter to More from my lord since the first examination but read it not. It had been agreed between them [the servants?] to deny any letters being sent between them. Thinks my lord gave many letters to George, and heard him tell George he might say he never carried any letters on the King's business.' At a later examination Wilson said that 'Fisher wrote a letter to More, which was not sealed or closed, and told him, if George was sober, to give it him to be delivered, which he did. Knows nothing of the contents.' And later, 'Thinks that letters have passed between Fisher and More since the last examination for he saw George bring his Master a letter, and afterwards cast it in the fire.'[1]

John Fisher was questioned on 12 June by Thomas Bedyll and Richard Layton. The answers were written down and each page signed by Fisher. His reply when questioned about the letters must be given in full.

There hath been letters sent between him and Master More to and fro upon a four or thereabouts from either of them to other, since they came to the Tower, touching the matters specified in these interrogatories. And, declaring the contents and effect of the same as far as he can remember, saith, that he remembered not the effect of any of the letters that either he sent to More, or that he received of Master

[1] For the interrogations, see *L.P.* Vol. 8, Nos 856, 858 and 867. The replies of Fisher and More are here given in full and not in the *L.P.* summaries.

More before the first being of the council here with this examined, but he doth well remember that there were letters sent to and fro between them and Master More before that time. And the first occasion of writing between them proceeded first of Master More, and now being better remembered, saith, that the effect of the first letter that Master More did write unto him after they came into the Tower was to know the effect of this deponent's answer which he had made to the council in the matter for the which he was first committed to the Tower. And then this respondent signified unto him by his letters what answer he had made them. Examined whether he doth remember the effect of any other letters that went between him and Master More before the first being of the council with them saith, No. And further examined what letters went between them since that time saith, that soon after that the council had been here first to examine this respondent, George, Master Lieutenant's servant, showed this examined a letter which Master More had addressed to his daughter Mistress Roper,[1] the effect whereof was this, that when the council had purposed [proposed] unto him the matter for the which they came for, he said that he would not dispute the King's title, and that Master Secretary gave him good words at his departure; and that is all he can remember of the effect of the same letter. And by the occasion of that letter this respondent wrote to Master More a letter to know a more clearness of his answer therein, which letter he did send him by the said George. And thereupon he received a letter again from the said Master More by the hands of the said George concerning his answer, but what the same was, he saith, he hath not in remembrance. And after a deliberate time, about a three or four days, this respondent calling to his remembrance the

---

[1] Perhaps *Rogers*, No 210.

words that his brother Robert Fisher had spoken unto him long before, viz. how that the Commons did stick and would not suffer the said statute to pass unless the word *maliciously* were put in it, wrote a letter containing the same words in effect, adding this 'if this word *maliciously* were put in the said statute, he thought it should be no danger if a man did answer to the question that was purposed unto him by the council after his own mind, so that he did not the same *maliciously*'. But, he saith, he nothing required or demanded in the said letters the advice or counsel of Master More therein, as he is sure that the same Master More himself would testify if he be examined. And thereupon, as this deponent thinketh, Master More supposing that this respondent's answer and his should be very nigh and like and that the council thereby would think that the one of them had taken light of the other, would, that the same suspicion should be avoided, and thereupon wrote a letter to this respondent accordingly.

Soon after the taking away of Master More's books from him, the said George came to this deponent and told him that Master More was in a peck of troubles, and that he desired to have either by writing or by word of mouth certain knowledge what answer this respondent had made to the council. And thereupon this respondent wrote unto him a letter that 'he had made his answer according to the statute which condemneth no man but him that speaketh *maliciously* against the king's title. And that the statute did compel no man to answer the question that was purposed him, and that he besought them that he should not be constrained to make further or other answer than the said statute did bind him but would suffer him to enjoy the benefits of the same statute.' Which was all the effect of the said letter as far as the deponent doth remember.

They [the letters] were all burned as soon as he read them and to the intent that the effects thereof should have been kept secret if it might be. For he was loth to be reproved of his promise made to Master Lieutenant that he would not do that thing for which he [the Lieutenant] might be put to blame. Albeit, if that there were more in the said letters than is before touched, he is sure it is nothing else but exhortation either of other to take patience in their adversity, and to call God for grace, and praying for their enemies, and nothing else that should hurt or offend any man earthly, as he saith.

John Fisher's difficulty in recalling details of the letters can be explained by his age and his greatly impaired health; he had been so critically ill during the previous winter that it seemed he could not recover.

Two days later, Thomas More was questioned. He said that

since he came to the Tower, he wrote divers scrolls or letters to Master Doctor Fisher, and received from him some other again; whereof the most part contained nothing else but comforting words from either to other, and declarations of the state that they were in, in their bodies, and giving of thanks for such meat and drink that the one had sent the other. But he saith, that he remembereth that upon a quarter of a year, to his remembrance, after the coming of this deponent to the Tower [i.e. about July 1534] this respondent wrote a letter to Master Fisher wherein he certified him that this examinat had refused the oath of succession; and never showed the Council, nor intended ever to show any other, the cause wherefore he did so refuse the same. And the said Master Fisher made him answer, by another letter, again, wherein he declared what answer he had made to the Council, and remembereth that this was part of the contents

thereof: 'how he had not refused to swear to the succession.'
And saith, that there were no other letters between them,
that any thing touched the King's business, laws or affairs,
till the Council came hither first of all to examine this
deponent upon the Act of Supreme Head. After which
examination, this examinat received a letter from Master
Fisher of this effect, viz. 'How he was desirous to know of
this respondent what answer he had made to the Council.'
And thereupon this respondent answered him by another
letter, other thus: 'My lord, I am determined to meddle of
no thing, but only to give my mind upon God, and the sum
of my whole study shall be, to think upon the Passion of
Christ, and my passage out of this world, with the dependen-
cies thereupon'. . . . Then, within a while after, he saith,
he received another letter from the said Master Fisher to this
effect: 'that he was informed that there was a word in the
statute, *maliciously*' and if it were so, that he thought thereby
'that a man, speaking nothing of malice, did not offend the
statute; and desired this respondent to show him, whether
he saw any otherwise in it'. And this respondent answered
him again, by another letter, shortly after, of this effect, viz.
'How this examinat took it to his thinking, as he did; but
the understanding or interpretation of the said statute should
neither be taken after his mind, nor after this deponent's
mind; and therefore it was not good for any man to trust to
any such thing.'

And saith farther, that other in his last letter, or in another
mean [intermediate] letter, between this and the first, he
wrote never, whether this examinat, confessing how he had
spoken to the Council, that he would meddle with nothing,
but would think on the Passion of Christ and his passage out
of the world, and that he had written the same words to
Master Fisher and fearing, lest it might happen him to speak

the same words, or like, in his answer to the Council, this examinat desired him to make his answer according to his own mind and to meddle with no such thing, as he had written unto him, lest he should give the Council occasion to wene [think] that there was some confederacy between them both.

Also saith, that since the last examination of him, this examinat did send Master Fisher word, by a letter that Mr Solicitor had showed him, that it was all one not to answer, or to say against the statute what a man would, as all the learned men of England would justify, as he said then; and therefore he said, he could reckon upon nothing else, but upon the uttermost; whereupon he prayed him to pray for this examinat, and he would again pray for him.

The next matter raised was a letter More had written to his daughter Margaret.[1] This does not bear directly on the exchange of notes between him and Fisher. He was then asked what had happened to the letters. He replied

that there is none of the said letters forthcoming, where he knoweth; but this examinat would have had George [Gold] to keep them, and George always said that there was no better keeper than the fire, and so burned them. And when he saw that he could not persuade George to keep them, he would have had George to show them, first of all to some trusty friend of his that could read, and if he saw that there were any matter of importance in them that he should carry the same to the Council and get the thanks himself first of any man therefore: and if there were none such matters in them that he should deliver them where he had directed. Yet the said George feared so (as he always said) his master, the Lieutenant, which had charged him highly that he should

[1] The passage is printed on page 103 of my *Margaret Roper*.

meddle with no such matters, lest he would have been extremely displeased with him, if he had seen that he had done anything were it never of so small importance, against his commandment, and therefore would he needs burn them.

More was then asked what was the intention of his letters to Fisher. It seems a pointless question, but More gave the simple answer, 'Considering they were both in one prison, and for one cause, he was glad to send unto him and to hear from him again.'

It is interesting to note that apparently Rich himself had taken a letter from More to Fisher. One wonders what happened to George Gold. He himself had been the first to admit carrying letters from one prisoner to the other and his answers read as if he said so quite readily. No further record of him can be traced.

More's answer should be compared with the answer he gave at his trial; the report of the latter seems summary and probably does not give his full meaning. In a trial today his replies at the interrogations with those of Fisher and the servants would be produced in court. The Indictment made use of More's warning to Fisher not to speak in similar terms to those he himself used.

The five interrogations are substantially in accord, making allowance for individual variations in details recalled. This result must have been disappointing to the Council, as there was nothing of a treasonous nature revealed. Correspondence between prisoners was a disciplinary offence within the Tower, though it seems to have been a not uncommon practice. Only if letters revealed criminal conspiracy would the matter be taken further, and the notes between Fisher and More could not bear that construction. The examiners had to accept the account of the contents given by the servants and their masters as all the letters had been burned by the cautious George, a fact that More regretted at his trial. For want of evidence from the letters the prosecution had to make use of words spoken by More on 12 May and by Fisher on 3 June, when they both described the Act as a two-edged sword. This suggested some kind of collaboration. More denied that there had been any such agreement and pointed out that their use of the same metaphor was accidental. It was not after all a recondite figure of speech. The report of Fisher's trial contains no allusion to the two-edged sword. Unless there is a gap in the observer's report in the *News Letter*, it seems that the court did not pursue the matter, but turned to the more significant Rich-More encounter.

Chapter 9

THE TRIAL: FOURTH COUNT

So far Harpsfield had drawn his material from the *News Letter* and the *Expositio*. The early accounts break off at this point and proceed at once to the jury's deliberations, thus saying nothing about the vital testimony of Richard Rich. For this Harpsfield had to turn to the memoir supplied to him by William Roper. Harpsfield bungled the transition from one authority to the other. He copied out, save for one introductory sentence, what Roper had written, namely:

> *And thus did Sir Thomas More easily cut and shake off such and like criminations, and among other things said that he would upon the Indictment have abiden in law, but that thereby he should have been driven to confess of himself the matter indeed, that was denial of the King's Supremacy, which he protested was untrue. Wherefore he thereto pleaded not guilty, and so reserved to himself advantage to be taken of the body of the matter after verdict to avoid the Indictment. And moreover added, that if these only odious terms, 'maliciously, traitorously and diabolically', were put out of the Indictment, he saw therein nothing justly to charge him.*

Roper, it must be remembered, was supplying what had been omitted from the *News Letter* and the *Expositio*; he did not therefore include More's replies to the first three counts. These early narratives did not give More's plea of

Not Guilty which must have come after the reading of the Indictment, so Roper introduced his additional material by making this point clear. In an orderly report of the trial this should have been put by Harpsfield in its proper place at the beginning instead of thrusting it between More's reply to the third and fourth counts. Harpsfield continued to copy Roper almost word for word.

> *Wherefore, for the last cast and refuge, to prove that Sir Thomas More was guilty of this treason, Master Rich was called for to give evidence to the jury upon his oath as he did. Against whom thus sworn, Sir Thomas More began in this wise to say, 'If I were a man, my lords, that did not regard an oath, I needed not, as it is well known in this place at this time nor in this case to stand here as an accused person. And if this oath of yours, Master Rich, be true, then pray I that I never see God in the face, which I would not say, were it otherwise, to win the whole world.' Then recited he to the Court the discourse of all their communication in the Tower, according to the truth.*

Rich's evidence would agree with the account given in the Indictment.[1] 'The discourse of all their communication' had already been given by Roper just before his account of the trial. This record was presumably reconstructed from the version More gave at the trial, as there was little opportunity for him to speak of it to anyone after Rich's visit on 12 June; from that date More had been more strictly confined and his books removed; the servants were probably too frightened after their interrogations to act as go-betweens. More's letter to Margaret dated 3 June was his last until the eve of his execution. There is a letter

1 See above, p. 68.

to Antonio Bonvisi[1] that was probably written during the last weeks of his imprisonment, but as it opened with the sentence, 'I shall not have long liberty to write unto you', it was probably written before his stricter confinement. We have, therefore, to depend on the Indictment, on More's reply to it, and on a manuscript that has hitherto escaped notice, for an understanding of the point at issue. Roper's account of the conversation was as follows:

Shortly hereupon, Master Rich, afterwards Lord Rich, then newly made the King's Solicitor, Sir Richard Southwell, and one Master Palmer, servant to the Secretary, were sent to Sir Thomas More into the Tower to fetch away his books from him. And while Sir Richard Southwell and Master Palmer were busy in the trussing up of his books, Master Rich, pretending friendly talk with him, among other things, of a set course, as it seemed, said thus unto him:

'Forasmuch as it is well known, Master More, that you are a man both wise and well learned as well in the laws of the Realm as otherwise, I pray you therefore, sir, let me be so bold as of good will to put unto you this case. Admit there were, sir,' quoth he, 'an Act of Parliament that all the Realm should take me for King. Would not you, Master More, take me for King?'

'Yes, sir,' quoth Sir Thomas More, 'that would I.'

'I put case further,' quoth Master Rich, 'that there were an Act of Parliament that all the Realm should take me for Pope. Would not you then, Master More, take me for Pope?'

'For answer, sir,' quoth Sir Thomas More, 'to your first case, the Parliament may well, Master Rich, meddle with the state of temporal Princes. But to make answer to your other

[1] *Rogers*, No 217.

cause, I will put this case—suppose the Parliament would make a law that God should not be God. Would you then, Master Rich, say that God were not God?'

'No, sir,' quoth he, 'that would I not, since no Parliament may make any such law.'

'No more,' said Sir Thomas More, as Master Rich reported him, 'could the Parliament make the King Supreme Head of the Church.'

At this point it will be useful to describe the manuscript to which reference has just been made.[1] It does not seem to have been previously examined by More's biographers, including myself. There is only a brief note on it in *Letters and Papers* (Vol. 8, No 814, 2, ii) with a cross-reference to the Indictment. I assumed that the document was a draft of the relevant part of the Indictment, but when I came to look at it, I found it had an importance of its own. The dilapidated condition of the two sheets, due to damp or rats, is discouraging, but enough can be deciphered to make sense. It is not dated; it may with some confidence be said to come between the conversation and the drawing up of the Indictment. It is therefore the earliest record of what was said. The document opens with a list of those present on 12 June 1535, when More's books were removed and he was more strictly confined. Sir Edmund Walsingham, Lieutenant of the Tower, was accompanied by Sir Richard Rich, Solicitor-General, Richard Southwell, and two servants whose Christian names are not given, Palmer and Berleght.[2] For the purposes of carrying out the Council's instructions, the presence of the Lieutenant of

---

[1] The P.R.O. reference is, S.P. 2/Folio R, folios 24, 25.
[2] *L.P.* reads 'Derleght', but the initial letter looks more like a B.

the Tower was sufficient; More must therefore have been put on his guard when he saw the Solicitor-General.

The conversation as recorded in this document opened with the passage in the Indictment in which More said, 'Your conscience will save you and my conscience will save me.' Then comes a fuller version of Rich's remark. 'Whereupon the said Richard . . . said to the said More, "Sir, for me to give you advice or counsel being a . . . experience, learning and wisdom, it were like as if a man should take . . . of water and cast it in Thames by cause it should be . . ." ' This well-oiled compliment (it is easy to guess the idea in spite of the gaps) is followed, as in the Indictment, by Rich's statement, 'Sir, protesting with you that I have no commission or commandment to . . . with you of the matter ye wot of, nevertheless with your favour I ask . . . you this case . . .' Then comes the hypothetical case of Parliament declaring Rich to be King. More's reply, as far as it is legible here, is on the lines of the Indictment.

According to Roper, the next 'case' was 'that all the realm should take me for Pope'. There is no mention of this in the document. Perhaps Rich thought it not tactful to mention the Pope in a report that might be seen by the King. The document goes on to give More's case of Parliament decreeing that 'God were not God', thus emphasizing that there are limits to its powers. Here unfortunately there is a considerable lacuna so we cannot be sure of the exact wording used by Rich; the word 'England' can be deciphered. More's reply in the best-preserved part of the document shows that Rich had put the question of the Supremacy. 'Whereunto the said More said that the cases were not like by cause that a King . . . y be made by

Parliament and a King deprived by Parliament to which act any . . . Subjects being of a Parliament may give his consent but to the case . . . a Subject can not be bound by cause he cannot give his cause [consent?] . . . him . . . Parliament. Saying further that although the King were accepted in England yet most utter parts [i.e. outer or foreign countries] do not affirm the same.'

We now come to the last passage of the report, and it is this that is of importance, as it adds to previous records, being neither in the Indictment nor in Roper's account. Rich's final words to More according to this document were as follows:

> 'Well, Sir, God comfort you, for I see your mind will not change which I fear will be very dangerous to you for I suppose your concealment to the question that hath been asked of you is as high offence as other that hath . . . And thus Jesu send you better grace.'

How are we to read this passage? It may be read as a warning to More that if he persisted in his 'concealment' this silence would be regarded as a serious offence; actually it became the first count in the Indictment. But it surely implies also that More had not revealed to Rich his full opinion on the Supremacy; he had gone so far as to say 'although the King were accepted as Supreme Head in England yet most utter parts do not affirm the same'. This, however, was not a categorical denial of the King's new title. The jury may have felt that it went far enough to convict him.

It may be noted that no actually incriminating words were quoted in English in the Indictment. In three earlier sections the words spoken were given in English. So, too, in the Indictment of John Fisher, his words were quoted in English: 'The King our sovereign lord is not Supreme Head in earth of the Church of England', words that he had been trapped into saying, in conversation with Rich on an occasion that Fisher thought was privileged. The final words given by Roper, 'No more could Parliament make the King Supreme Head of the Church', are not given in the Indictment. The meaning of what was there stated is not at first apparent, as the phrasing is clumsy. In translation the passage reads: 'The King can be made or unmade by Parliament, to which every subject being at the Parliament may give his consent; but as to the Supremacy, the subject cannot be bound, since he cannot give his consent in Parliament, and though the King be accepted as such in Parliament, there are many other countries that do not agree.' The argument, as here worded, is far from clear; it looks as though More had said that the people can give consent to the succession through Parliament, but cannot give their consent to the Supremacy through Parliament. If they can give consent to the succession, why not also to the Supremacy? Some amplification is here needed. The people in Parliament have the right and power to settle the succession; that is within their competence; but the people in Parliament have not the right nor the power to bestow the Supremacy on the King, as it is something no single country can decide; it is a matter for other countries as well. Roper's version, 'as Master Rich reported him', is more damaging. Had More, in fact, said that Parliament could not make the King Supreme Head he would have been placing his own head on the block, a fact of which he was well aware.[1]

His defence was that he had not made any such statement, and he went on to point out that it was plainly ridiculous to imagine that he would have said such a thing to a visitor when he had time and again refused to give any answer on that very point to members of the Council itself. Two days after the conversation with Rich, More was again questioned on behalf of the Council. Three questions were put to him.

1. Whether he would obey the King as Supreme Head?
He can make no answer.
2. Whether he will acknowledge the King's marriage with Queen Anne to be lawful, and that with lady Catherine invalid?
Never spoke against it, 'nor thereunto can make no answer'.
3. Where it was objected to him that by the said statute he, as one of the King's subjects, is bound to answer the said question and recognize the King as Supreme Head, like all other subjects?
He can make no answer.

Did the Council hope that he would repeat the words he was alleged to have spoken to Rich two days earlier? Or were they not satisfied with what he was said to have said to Rich? There seems no point in the first question if More had already said 'No' to Rich's inquiry. He again refused to answer the direct question; they therefore had to fall back on Rich's report for the less definite statement.

[1] In actual fact, Parliament did not *make* Henry Supreme Head. It has already been pointed out that the Act was declaratory; Parliament accepted a position assumed by the King with the consent of the Convocations.

At the trial Thomas More said,

'*In good faith, Master Rich, I am sorrier for your perjury than for mine own peril. And you shall understand that neither I, nor any man else to my knowledge, ever took you to be a man of such credit as in any matter of importance I, or any other, would at any time vouchsafe to communicate with you. And I, as you know, of no small while have been acquainted with you and your conversation, who have known you from your youth hitherto; for we long dwelled both in one parish together, where, as yourself can well tell (I am sorry you compel me so to say) you were esteemed very light of your tongue, a common liar, a great dicer and of no commendable fame. And so in your house at the Temple, where hath been your chief bringing up, were you likewise accounted.*

'*Can it therefore seem likely to your honourable Lordships that I would, in so weighty a case, so unadvisedly overshoot myself as to trust Master Rich (a man of me always reputed for one of so little trust, as your Lordships have heard) so far above my Sovereign Lord the King or any of his noble Councillors, that I would unto him utter the secrets of my conscience touching the King's Supremacy, the special point and only mark at my hands so long sought for, a thing which I never did, nor never would, after the Statute thereof made, reveal either to the King's Highness himself or to any of his honourable Councillors, as it is not unknown to your honours, at sundry several times sent from His Grace's own person unto the Tower to me for none other purpose? Can this in your judgments, my lords, seem likely to be true?*'

More then claimed that even had he spoken the alleged words, they were in course of easy conversation, 'in putting cases' as in the moots in the Inns of Court; they could not be construed as malicious in such circumstances. He then drew a distinction between *malitia* meaning badness or vice, and *malevolentia* meaning ill will, spite.

'*And yet if I had so done indeed, my lords, as Master Rich hath sworn, seeing it was spoken but in familiar secret talk, nothing affirming, and only in putting cases, without other displeasant circumstances, it cannot justly be taken to be spoken maliciously, for where there is no malice, there can be no malicious offence. And never think, my lords, that so many worthy Bishops, so many honourable personages, and so many other worshipful, virtuous, wise and well-learned men as at the making of that law were in the Parliament assembled, ever meant to have any man punished by death in whom there could be found no malice, taking malitia for malevolentia; for if malitia be generally taken for sin, no man is there then that thereof can excuse himself, Quia si dixerimus quod peccatum non habemus, nosmet ipsos seducimus, et veritas in nobis non est.[1] And only this word "maliciously" is in this Statute material, as this term "forcibly" is in the Statute of Forcible Entry. By which Statute, if a man enter peaceably and put not his adversary out forcibly, it is no offence, but if he put him out forcibly, then by that Statute it is an offence, and so shall he be punished by this term "forcibly".*'

Finally, he asked if it was conceivable that he who had been so favourably regarded and trusted by the King would speak maliciously against him?

'*Besides this, the manifold goodness of the King's Highness himself, that hath been so many ways my singular good Lord and Gracious Sovereign, that hath so dearly loved and trusted me (even at my very first coming unto his noble service with the dignity of his honourable Privy Council vouchsafing to admit me) and to offices of great credit and worship most liberally advanced me, and finally with that weighty room of His Grace's High Chancellor (the like whereof he never did to temporal man before)*'

---

[1] I John i. 8: 'If we say we have no sin, we deceive ourselves, and the truth is not in us.'

*next to his own royal person the highest officer of this noble
Realm, so far above my merits or qualities able and meet therefore
of his incomparable benignity honoured and exalted me, by the
space of twenty years and more shewing his continual favour towards me, and (until at mine own poor humble suit it pleased His
Highness, giving me licence with His Majesty's favour to bestow
the residue of my life for the provision of my soul in the service of
God, of his special goodness thereof to discharge and disburden
me) most benignly heaping honours continually more and more
upon me—all this His Highness's goodness, I say, so long thus
bountifully extended towards me, were in my mind, my lords,
matter sufficient to convince this slanderous surmise by this man so
wrongfully imagined against me.'*

In answer to More's charge of perjury, Rich called two
witnesses to testify to his version of the conversation.

*Master Rich, seeing himself so disproved, and his credit so
foully defaced, caused Sir Richard Southwell and Master Palmer,
that at the time of their communication were in the chamber with
them, to be sworn, what words had passed betwixt them. Whereupon Master Palmer, upon his deposition, said that he was so
busy about the trussing up of Sir Thomas More's books in a sack,
that he took no heed to their talk. Sir Richard Southwell likewise,
upon his deposition, said that because he was appointed only to
look to the conveyance of his books, he gave no ear unto them.*

*After this there were many other reasons, not now in my
remembrance, by Sir Thomas More in his own defence alleged, to
the discredit of Master Rich's foresaid evidence, and proof of the
clearness of his own conscience.*

Richard Southwell,[1] aged thirty and already wealthy,
was Sheriff of Norfolk, and tutor to Cromwell's son

[1] He was the grandfather of Robert Southwell, S. J., poet and martyr.

Gregory. He seems to have been in charge of the 'trussing up' of the books. Palmer is referred to as one of Cromwell's servants in a letter of May 1535;[1] he and Berleght (of whom nothing further is discoverable) would do the actual parcelling. More and Rich would be standing apart in conversation and the others would be little likely to hear much except an occasional phrase. When Southwell and Palmer said they 'took little heed' or 'gave no ear', they were probably speaking the truth. Rich must have expected them to confirm his version. Why did they refuse to do so? The simplest explanation may be the true one; they preferred not to perjure themselves. The later career of Southwell, who prospered from reign to reign, was to show that he had few scruples, but this must not rob him of the credit of having spoken the truth at the trial. The jury does not seem to have given much weight to the failure of the two men to back up the Solicitor-General.

[1] *L.P.*, Vol. 8, No 732. His identification with Sir John Palmer (*Harpsfield*, p. 348) is an error.

Chapter 10

GUILTY

HARPSFIELD, following Roper, made the bare statement, 'All which notwithstanding, the jury found him guilty.' The *News Letter* gave more detail.

> Then were called by an usher twelve men according to the custom of the country, and these articles were given to them so that they could consult and judge if the said Sir Thomas More had maliciously contravened the said Act or not. Who, after they had retired a quarter of an hour, returned before the lords and ordinary judges and pronounce GUILTY, that is condemned or worthy of death. At once was his judgment pronounced by the Chancellor according to the tenor of the new law.

The *Expositio* and *Novitates* have similar accounts.

The names of the jurymen are on record but none can be identified; two had been on the jury at the trial of John Fisher. There were two knights, five esquires and five gentlemen.[1] As we know nothing of their deliberations, it is pointless to argue about their decision. Presumably they accepted Rich's evidence. They must have been overawed by a Commission that included the Chancellor, the

[1] The paucity of records of trials at that period makes it impossible to answer such a question as, 'was the Indictment translated into English for the benefit of the jurymen, not all of whom, if any, would have an easy command of Latin?'

two Chief Justices, the Chief Baron and other judges, together with Anne Boleyn's father, her uncle and her
brother, the King's brother-in-law, and, not least, Thomas
Cromwell. It would have been out-of-keeping with the
times for the jury to have brought in a verdict of Not
Guilty. Thomas More did not expect acquittal.

Harpsfield's account continues.

> *And incontinent upon their verdict the Lord Chancellor, for
> that matter chief commissioner, beginning to proceed in judgment
> against him, Sir Thomas More said unto him, 'My lord, when I
> was toward the law, the manner in such case was to ask the
> prisoner, before judgment, why judgment should not be given
> against him.' Whereupon the Lord Chancellor, staying his judg-
> ment, wherein he had partly proceeded demanded of him what he
> was able to say to the contrary; who in this sort most humbly made
> answer.*

The usual procedure can be illustrated from a report of
the trial of Sir Christopher Blunt and four others in March
1600.[1] They were tried before seven commissioners and
the judges. The record reads:

> Now the Jury went out to argue upon the Verdict, which
> after half an hour's time or more, they brought in, and found
> every of the five prisoners severally Guilty of High Treason.
> The Verdict being entered, and the Jury discharged, the
> Queen's Serjeant prayed Judgement. The Lord Chief Justice
> then demanded of the prisoners what they had to say for
> themselves why judgment should not be given against
> them.

Audley's lapse may have been due to inexperience, or

[1] *State Trials* (Cobbett, 1809), Vol. I, p. 1410.

perhaps to nervousness in dealing with a predecessor of high reputation. It may possibly have been that the King issued instructions that More should 'not use many words', as he did before the execution. To stay a convicted prisoner from speaking against the verdict was to rob him of a cherished privilege of unburdening his mind. The speech More made was a carefully thought-out statement, for at last he could break the silence he had imposed on himself.

A comparison between the account in Harpsfield and that in the *News Letter* will be helpful at this point.

HARPSFIELD	NEWS LETTER
Judgement Interrupted	**Judgement Pronounced**
MORE: No single realm can legislate for the Universal Church.	No Prince can be Supreme Head of Church.

AUDLEY: Do you put your opinion higher than that of all other in the Realm?

MORE: No Prince can be Supreme Head of Church. Supported by Fathers and Saints of all times.	Supported by Fathers and Saints of all times.

NORFOLK: This reveals your malice.

MORE: Marriage true origin of prosecution	⎧ No single realm can legislate for the Universal Church. Marriage true origin of prosecution.
Judgement Pronounced May King be given good counsel.	⎩ May King be given good counsel.

It will be seen that the two accounts cover the same ground, but with the arguments in a different order. The *News Letter* is compressed and, without the Harpsfield-Roper version, it would be difficult to get the full value out of the argument. We should lack the splendid opening passage which is the key to More's position.

'Seeing that I see ye are determined to condemn me (God knoweth how) I will now in discharge of my conscience speak my

mind plainly and freely touching my Indictment and your Statute, withal.

'*And forasmuch as this Indictment is grounded upon an Act of Parliament directly repugnant to the laws of God and his Holy Church, the supreme Government of which, or of any part where- of, may no temporal Prince presume by any law to take upon him, as rightfully belonging to the See of Rome, a spiritual pre- eminence by the mouth of our Saviour himself, personally present upon earth, only to St Peter and his successors, Bishops of the same See, by special prerogative granted; it is therefore in law, amongst Christian men, insufficient to charge any Christian man.*' *And for proof thereof, like as among divers other reasons and authorities he declared that this Realm, being but one member and small part of the Church, might not make a particular law dis- agreeable with the general law of Christ's Universal Catholic Church, no more than the City of London, being but one poor member in respect of the whole Realm, might make a law against an Act of Parliament to bind the whole Realm. So further shewed he that it was contrary both to the laws and statutes of our own land yet unrepealed, as they might evidently perceive in Magna Charta,* Quod Anglicana ecclesia libera sit et habeat jura sua integra, et libertates suas illaesas.[1] *And also contrary to the sacred oath which the King's Highness himself, and every other Christian Prince always with great solemnity received at their coronations, alleging, moreover, that no more might this Realm of England refuse obedience to the See of Rome than might the child refuse obedience to his own natural father. For as St Paul said of the Corinthians, 'I have regenerated you, my children in Christ,'[2] so might St Gregory, Pope of Rome, of whom by St Augustine his messenger, we first received the Christian faith, of us*

---

[1] That the English Church shall be free, and shall have its rights un- diminished and its liberties unimpaired. (First clause of the Charter.)

[2] I Cor. iv, 15.

Englishmen truly say, 'You are my children, because I have given you everlasting salvation, a far higher and better inheritance than any carnal father can leave to his children, and by regeneration made you my spiritual children in Christ.'

More was here affirming an essential principle of 'Christ's Universal Catholic Church', as he liked to call it, a principle that has been part of Christian teaching since the foundation of the Church. There are limits set by Divine Law to the authority of princes and states. No single prince or state can legislate for the whole Church or, without injustice, demand of the individual anything contrary to Christian teaching. When the State goes beyond those limits, the individual Christian has a duty to obey conscience in consonance with the teaching of the Church rather than obey the State. In illustration of traditional teaching a quotation from St Thomas Aquinas may be given.

> Man is bound to obey secular rulers to the extent that the order of justice requires. For this reason if such rulers have no just title to power, but have usurped it, or if they command things to be done which are unjust, their subjects are not obliged to obey them, except perhaps in special cases, when it is a matter of avoiding scandal or some particular danger.

Few men have been as scrupulous as More in serving their king with complete faithfulness; his whole public life was evidence of a true loyalty to the King. Whatever More may have felt about the personal character of Henry, he did not allow this to affect his devotion to the Crown. This makes his final refusal of obedience all the more impressive. Moreover, he recognized that his decision had to be a personal one. When the verdict went against him, he felt liberated from this self-imposed restriction, and at last he could speak his mind.

We can see his protest as directed against the rapid extension of Royal and Parliamentary authority into a field that had hitherto been reserved to the Church. All the powers of the papacy were transferred to the Crown between 1533 and 1536. Not the least significant of the changes was the ban on the teaching of Canon Law in the universities. As yet the new Supreme Head had not attempted to define doctrine by declaration or statute, but that power was implicit in the revolution that had been effected. If men could no longer look to Rome, where could they look? Even the authority of the Convocations was in abeyance. It was one of the distinctions of More that, from the early days of the King's Matter, he had sensed how far the King might go, for few men had come to know Henry's disposition as he had done. Had he not warned Cromwell? 'Master Cromwell, you are now entered into the service of a most noble, wise and liberal prince. If you will follow my poor advice, you shall, in your counsel giving to his Grace, ever tell him what he ought to do, but never what he is able to do. So shall you show yourself a true faithful servant and a right worthy Councillor. For if the lion knew his own strength, hard were it for any man to rule him.' Cromwell chose to tell the King 'what he is able to do'.

Audley interrupted More's speech.

Then was it by the Lord Chancellor thereunto answered that seeing all the Bishops, Universities and best learned men of the

Realm had to this Act agreed, it was much marvel that he alone against them all would so stiffly stick thereat, and so vehemently argue there against. The which reason in effect the Bishop of Westminster also made against him, when he appeared before the Commissioners at Lambeth.

To this Sir Thomas More replied, saying that these seven years seriously and earnestly he had beset his studies and cogitations upon this point chiefly, among other, of the Pope's authority. 'Neither as yet', said he, 'have I chanced upon any ancient writer or doctor that so advanceth, as your Statute doth, the supremacy of any secular and temporal Prince. If there were no more but myself upon my side, and the whole Parliament upon the other, I would be sore afraid to lean to mine own mind only against so many. But if the number of Bishops and Universities be so material as your Lordships seemeth to take it, then see I little cause, my Lord, why that thing in my conscience should make any change. For I nothing doubt but that, though not in this Realm, yet in Christendom about, of these well-learned Bishops and virtuous men that are yet alive, they be not the fewer part that are of my mind therein. But if I should speak of those that are already dead, of whom many be now Holy Saints in heaven, I am very sure it is the far greater part of them that, all the while they lived, thought in this case that way that I think now, and therefore am I not bounden, my Lord, to conform my conscience to the Council of one Realm against the General Council of Christendom. For of the aforesaid holy Bishops I have for every Bishop of yours, above one hundred, and for one Council or Parliament of yours (God knoweth what manner of one), I have all the Councils made these thousand years. And for this one kingdom, I have all other Christian Realms.'

The only bishop who had maintained his opposition to the Supremacy was John Fisher. It was Thomas Cranmer who, in August 1529, suggested that opinions on the validity of the dispensation for Henry's first marriage should be obtained from the universities of Europe. Agents set out on this mission in the autumn of 1529 and sought, and bought, the desired opinions.

Harpsfield has conflated his sources in this passage to an unusual degree. His reference to the 'Bishop of Westminster' was a slip of the pen and is not serious. He should have written 'Abbot', as the diocese of Westminster was not formed until 1540 and was reabsorbed in that of London in 1550. The first and only bishop was Thomas Thirlby. The Abbot of Westminster was William Benson (Boston), who surrendered the Abbey in 1540 and had become its first Dean. He had been one of the Commissioners at Lambeth when More first refused the oath to the Succession.

The next passage must be analysed into its components.

HARPSFIELD

To this Sir Thomas More replied, saying that these seven years seriously and earnestly he had beset his studies and cogitations upon this point chiefly, among other, of the Pope's authority.

NEWS LETTER

'Neither as yet,' said he, 'have I chanced upon any ancient writer or doctor that so advanceth, as your Statute doth, the supremacy of any secular and temporal Prince.'

HARPSFIELD

'If there were no more but myself upon my side, and the whole Parliament upon the other, I would be sore afraid to lean to mine own mind only against so many.'

ROPER

But if the number of Bishops and Universities be so material as your Lordships seemeth to take it, then see I little cause, my Lord, why that thing in my conscience should make any change. For I nothing doubt but that, though not in this Realm, yet in Christendom about, of these well-learned Bishops and virtuous men that are yet alive, they be not the fewer part that are of my mind therein. But if I should speak of those that are already dead, of whom many be now Holy Saints in heaven, I am very sure it is the far greater part of them that, all the while they lived, thought in this case that way that I think now, and therefore am I not bounden, my Lord, to conform my conscience to the Council of one Realm against the General Council of Christendom.'

NEWS LETTER

'For of the aforesaid holy Bishops I have for every Bishop of yours, above one hundred, and for one Council or Parliament of yours (God knoweth what manner of one), I have all the Councils made these thousand years. And for this one kingdom, I have all other Christian Realms.'

Harpsfield's opening sentence is misleading. There were two distinct problems that More had studied:

(1) the nature of the Supremacy of the Apostolic See, and
(2) whether a secular prince could be Supreme Head.

He had been led to consider the first when Henry asked him to edit the *Assertio Septem Sacramentorum* about 1520.[1] More then advised the King to modify his references to

[1] *Roper*, pp. 67–68.

the authority of the Pope. The problem became acute when Henry first expressed his doubts on the validity of his marriage with Catherine; this was in 1527. The consideration of the power of the Pope to grant dispensations inevitably led to an examination of papal authority. The second problem arose in 1531, when the Convocations were asked to accept Henry as Supreme Head of the Church of England.

In a letter to Cromwell of March 1534,[1] More said that he had studied the first of these two problems, the Primacy of the Pope, 'these ten years and more'. This takes us back to the period following More's discussion with the King about his book. The period of seven years mentioned at the trial referred to the second problem, the King's new title of Supreme Head. This points to 1528, but this was the best part of two years before the matter came before the Convocations. There is no record of the King having discussed the matter with More, but that does not rule out the possibility that he did do so; there is, in fact, little evidence of when or how the notion got into Henry's head. As Chancellor, from October 1529, More should have known of the King's intentions, but Henry may have kept his counsel. It may equally well be that it was a sudden impulse rather than a carefully considered policy.

The length of time devoted by More to these grave questions is evidence of the seriousness with which he considered them. His letter to Cromwell of March 1534 confirms this, and the letter he wrote to Dr Nicholas Wilson[2] when they were both in the Tower supplies

[1] *Rogers*, No 199.
[2] *Rogers*, No 208.

additional details. 'I cannot now tell', he wrote, 'how many years, of all those that I talked with of the matter and with whom I most conferred those places of Scripture and of the old holy Doctors that touched either the one side or the other, with the councils and laws on either side, that speak thereof also, the most, as I trow you wot well, was yourself.' More's decision, therefore, was the result of prolonged consideration and consultation, and, we may be certain, of prayer.

Harpsfield's second interpolation on the weight of Parliament's opinion is not out of keeping with More's argument, but it has only Harpsfield's authority. This cannot be rejected out of hand; some of those who had been at the trial were still alive when Harpsfield was writing, and, as we have seen, he enjoyed the companionship of the More exiles during his years at Louvain only fifteen years after the trial. From them and from unrecorded sources he may have gathered these other remarks; how far these were hearsay or first-hand evidence it is impossible to know.

One phrase in Harpsfield's account has led to a misunderstanding of what More must have said: 'for one Council or Parliament of yours (God knoweth what manner of one) . . .' Harpsfield was following the *News Letter*: 'et pour ung vostre parlement, Dieu scait quel . . .' This reads in the *Expositio*, 'pro unico vestro concilio, quod quale sit Deus novit'. The *Novitates* reads, 'ac pro uno consilio ac decreto vestro (quod quale sit Deus Optimus Maximus novit)'—'as for your Parliament and your statute . . .' This is certainly a preferable reading and is far more likely to be what More actually said. He was not

commenting on the Parliament, but on the statute. Harpsfield's reading has produced an unnecessary amount of
heat about the 'packing' of the 1529–36 House of Commons. It was originally no more 'packed' than previous
Parliaments; the influence of the Crown had always been
used, and for several more centuries would be used, to
bring in members likely to be favourable to the sovereign's
wishes; that influence was never absolute and many members could be described as independent of the Crown.[1]
The length of the 1529 Parliament meant that an increase
in the number of royal nominees could be obtained, and
as soon as Cromwell was in effective control the business
of using Crown influence was carried out more systematically. Deaths and withdrawals gave Cromwell oppor-
tunities to exercise pressure on the patrons of constituen-
cies; thus in January 1534 there were as many as forty
seats to be filled out of some four hundred. The creation
of new boroughs was another way of using influence.
Thomas More was not likely to complain of a characteristic of Parliament that was not an innovation. The Commons were never completely subservient, and it may be
noted that five of More's near relatives were members:
his brother-in-law, John Rastell, his three sons-in-law,
William Roper, Giles Heron and William Daunce, as well
as Sir Giles Alington, the husband of his stepdaughter.
Parliament, in fact, regrettable as it may have been, faith-
fully represented the prevailing anti-clerical (not anti-
Catholic) tone of society and that explains why Henry and
Cromwell had little difficulty in getting the legislation

[1] It could be maintained that the House of Commons was more venal
in the eighteenth than in the sixteenth century.

they desired. More's objection was to the Act of Supremacy as being outside the competence of the King and Parliament of a single realm, since it affected the Universal Church.

The Duke of Norfolk considered that this argument showed More's malicious intention.

> *Then answered the Duke of Norfolk. 'We now plainly perceive that ye are maliciously bent.' 'Nay, nay,' quoth Sir Thomas More, 'very and pure necessity, for the discharge of my conscience, enforceth me to speak so much. Wherein I call and appeal to God, whose only sight pierceth into the very depth of man's heart, to be my witness. Howbeit, it is not for this supremacy so much that ye seek my blood, as for that I would not condescend to the marriage.',*

The last sentence recalls the opening passage in Harpsfield's version of More's defence. It was then pointed out that the reference to the marriage seemed out of place at that point. Here it comes abruptly, so there may be some displacement again. The *News Letter* only brings in the marriage question in this reply to Norfolk. The *Ordo* goes further and introduces a reference to John the Baptist's protest at the marriage of Herod to Herodias, his brother Philip's wife. This is not given in any of the other documents. It was a parallel drawn by John Fisher in his defence of Queen Catherine at Blackfriars in 1529, but it is unlikely that the writer of the *Ordo* could have known that. This interpolation strengthens one's impression that the *Ordo* was a write-up, rather than a strict reproduction of primary material.

> *When now, Sir Thomas More, for the avoiding of his Indictment, had taken as many exceptions as he thought meet, and*

many more reasons than I can now remember alleged, the Lord Chancellor, loath to have the burden of that judgment wholly to depend upon himself, there openly asked the Lord FitzJames, then Lord Chief Justice of the King's Bench, and joined in Commission with him, whether this Indictment were sufficient or not. Who like a wise man answered, 'My lords all, by St Julian (that was ever his oath) I must needs confess that, if the Act of Parliament be lawful, then the Indictment is good enough.' Whereupon the Lord Chancellor said to the rest of the lords, 'Lo, my lords, you hear what my Lord Chief Justice saith.' And so immediately gave he judgment against him.

We owe this knowledge of the curious FitzJames incident to Roper. Audley seems again to have been rather unsure of himself. It was a bit late to ask if the Indictment was valid. FitzJames replied with a series of negative qualifications that suggest that he, too, had been thrown off his balance. Can we interpret this and Audley's earlier stumble as signs of tension in the court, of uneasiness at the task set the Commissioners in judging such a notable prisoner?

The actual judgment is not given. More was condemned to be drawn to Tyburn from the Tower, to be hanged and quartered. But, according to Roper, the giving of judgment did not end the trial.

After which ended, the Commissioners yet further courteously offered him, if he had anything else to allege for his defence, to grant him favourable audience. Who answered, 'More have I not to say, my Lords, but that like the Blessed Apostle St Paul as we read in the Acts of the Apostle, was present and consented to the death of St Stephen, and kept their clothes that stoned him to death, and yet be they now both twain Holy Saints in heaven, and

*shall continue there friends together for ever, so I verily trust,
and shall therefore right heartily pray, that though your lordships
have now here in earth been judges to my condemnation, we may
hereafter in heaven merrily all meet together, to our everlasting
salvation. And thus I desire Almighty God to preserve and defend
the King's Majesty and to send him good counsel.'*

Roper is our only authority for this invitation from the
Commissioners to More to speak again after judgment
had been given. It was an irregular proceeding if it happened in this way, yet it is difficult to believe that an
experienced lawyer like Roper would have been mistaken. The *News Letter* and other early narratives make
this passage continuous with More's reply to Norfolk.
Harpsfield took the final sentence from the *News Letter*;
in the *Expositio*, however, the last word is wrongly given
as 'counsellors' instead of 'counsel'.

We can see More standing, as it were, between the
Middle Ages and the New Age. There had always been
problems of demarcating the respective spheres of Church
and State, of Pope and King; at times there had been angry
disputes. In our own history we can think of Anselm and
Becket. Indeed, More could have used Anselm's own
words: 'I am not afraid of banishment, or torments, or
death; for all these, God strengthening me, my heart is
ready in obedience to the Apostolic See, and for the
liberty of my mother the Church.' Apart from these more
spectacular clashes, Church and State in England managed
to find a working compromise, and such statutes as Pro-
visors and Praemunire were not systematically enforced;
one might say they were there 'in terrorem'. At no point,
however, had it ever been contemplated that the King

should usurp the universal authority of the Apostolic See in matters that affected the spiritual welfare of the people. More was protesting at what seemed to him to be an invasion of the rights of 'Christ's Universal Catholic Church' by the King or by King and Parliament. On one level it can be regarded as a constitutional issue, as it concerned the legitimate functions of a secular legislative body. King and Parliament had their way and the Church of England today is subject to the ultimate opinion of Parliament.[1]

More was fighting a losing battle, but it was one that in all conscience he could not refuse.

[1] The most striking example in this century was when Parliament (in particular the Commons) in December 1927 refused to sanction a revision of the Book of Common Prayer that was desired by the Church.

Chapter 11

THE ISSUES

In the course of analysing Harpsfield's account of the trial of Sir Thomas More a number of comments have been made designed to bring out the significance of each stage. It seems desirable to draw these detached remarks together, even at the risk of some repetition, so that the larger implications may not be overlooked.

We may first note some features of the trial. The Treason Act of November 1534 had created new forms of treason; among these was that of denying any of his titles to the King. To say that he was not the rightful King could with some justice be interpreted as evidence of treasonable intention, though merely 'saying' without consequent 'doing' was a harsh construction. As we have seen, the qualifying word 'maliciously' might as well have been left out of the Act. The title 'Supreme Head in earth of the Church of England' was of a different character from other titles. It was a revolutionary innovation that went far beyond safeguarding the Crown, since it involved the whole problem of the relation of the Universal Church under the Pope and the King of one country. To accept the King's new title was to deny the Pope's age-long position as head of the Church. It was ironic that the papally bestowed title of 'Defender of the Faith' was retained.

The judges were not concerned with the justification

of these unprecedented titles; they had to interpret the new law. Fisher's case had offered no complications; the words of his rejection of the Supremacy had been quoted in his indictment and he did not deny having spoken them. More's position was far from simple. It had not been possible to quote any categorical statement by him against the King's Supremacy. His silence had to be interpreted as malicious refusal; his exchanges of notes with Fisher, and the report (as given in the Indictment) of the conversation with Rich were not in themselves positive evidence of his treason under the new law. The judges had to make the best they could of a weak case. There could be no question of an acquittal. More would not have been brought to trial had not the King willed it. He was already imprisoned for life under the Act of Attainder. It may be hazarded that some of the judges would have preferred that no further action should be taken. Our thoughts naturally turn to Thomas Cromwell. It is clear that during the earlier period of More's imprisonment, Cromwell was anxious to win his compliance with the King's wishes, for the younger man had a regard for his senior and they both enjoyed the friendship of Antonio Bonvisi. Once, however, Cromwell realized that the King desired More's death, he accepted the inevitable. The responsibility for the deaths of John Fisher and Thomas More must be laid squarely on the shoulders of Henry VIII; there was a strain of malignancy in his character that drove him beyond the needs of policy when his will was thwarted. More was doubtless right in saying that his failure to support the King in his marriage troubles was at the root of what became a persecution.

Probably no man appreciated Henry's character more justly than did Thomas More. There had been a time when they were more intimate than Wolsey himself had been, or, later, than Cromwell was to be. This halcyon period when King Henry and Queen Catherine enjoyed the society of Thomas More had provided an unequalled opportunity for knowing the King's nature. More's remark to Roper, 'If my head could win a castle in France, it should not fail to go', and his warning to Cromwell, 'If the lion knew his own strength, hard were it for any man to rule him', were evidence of More's insight. To us it may seem a paradox that, in spite of this knowledge, and in spite of his bitter experience of the King's malevolence, More could to the very end declare himself to be the King's good servant, and mean it. The paradox is resolved if we remind ourselves of the view of kingship that More shared with his contemporaries. As this has a direct bearing on his attitude towards the Supremacy, it calls for consideration.

It is a commonplace to say that the thirty or more years of factious internecine wars, usually called the Wars of the Roses, that ended with the battle of Bosworth in 1485, predisposed the nation to accept firm government under any king who could supply it. This was not, however, a desire that was peculiar to England; it was to be found in France and elsewhere. The growing importance of a merchant class intent on peaceful commerce also favoured strong government. Henry VII was able to provide it; he was fortunately spared for twenty-four years in which, with great skill and wisdom (or cunning, as some called it), he was able to re-establish the monarchy as the source of law and order. The prestige of the monarchy rose in spite of grumblings towards the end of the reign. The second Tudor was a magnificent creature whose very presence embodied the dignity of monarchy. He was not as wise as his father, but he ruled as no king had ever ruled in England before him. By 1535 he was kingship incarnate, and few dared to frustrate his will. Loyalty to the monarchy carried with it notions that had been part of medieval thinking about kingship; it retained the aura surrounding one who had been consecrated and anointed as the representative of God.

> *Not all the water in the rough rude sea*
> *Can wash the balm off from an anointed king.*

This view was qualified by the belief that a king was not above natural or divine law,[1] nor could he break his coronation oath by ignoring the common and customary law of the land. The Tudors enjoyed a wide prerogative, but they were expected to seek the consent of the people in Parliament when fresh taxes or new laws were contemplated. There was another limitation to absolutism. The doctrine of the two swords was universally accepted; in purely spiritual matters, the Church was supreme.

All this was part of Thomas More's thinking, though it would be difficult to give quotations to establish the claim; his conduct provides the evidence. It is notable that he avoided political questions in his writings after he became a councillor; his letters throw no light on his views of contemporary affairs, nor did Roper do more than note a

[1] The terms may be regarded as almost interchangeable, as they were not always kept distinct by medieval writers. 'Fundamental law' and the 'Law of Reason' are sometimes used, but without precision or clear distinction.

rare dictum. It may seem strange that the author of *Utopia*
made no further excursions into political speculation. The
second part of that book, the description of Utopia, has
proved a stimulus to thought, with the result that some
queer notions have been fathered on More. It should not,
perhaps, be taken too seriously; it was a somewhat aca-
demic exercise enjoyed by a few friends in Flanders, of
whom Erasmus, for a few days, was one, in devising the
polity of an ideal republic. The first part of *Utopia* is a
very different product. It was composed on More's return
to England, when Erasmus was his visitor for a while.
This part pulses with life in contrast to the rather frigid
description of the second part. More was now dealing
with problems of social justice that confronted him in his
everyday experience. The portion that concerns us here
is the discussion with Hythlodaye on whether the philo-
sopher should enter the service of his prince. It was an
immediate issue with More, as the King wanted him to
become a member of his Council. Speaking for himself,
More said, 'Suppose wrong opinions cannot be plucked
up by the root, and you cannot cure, as you would wish,
vices of long standing, yet you must not on that account
abandon the ship of state and desert it in a storm because
you cannot control the winds. . . . What you cannot
turn to good, you must make as little bad as you can.'
When he did enter the service of the King he interpreted
this as meaning that he would give the best advice he
could in the Council or privately to the King, but that
he must not rock the boat. Outside the Council Chamber he
kept silent on matters of policy. Ambassadors complained
that they could get nothing out of him, and one said that

however skilfully he framed his questions More as skilfully avoided giving any information on state affairs. We have seen how his opinion on Henry's marriage problem was given to the King personally. He later wrote, 'After this [i.e. after he had given the King his final opinion] did I never nothing more therein, nor never any word wrote I therein to the impairing of his Grace's part neither before nor after, nor any man else by my procurement.'[1]

When on 30 March 1531 the collected opinions of the universities on the King's predicament were read to the Lords and More was asked for his opinion, he replied that his views were known to the King. As Chancellor he delivered the same opinions to the Commons, but again he refrained from making any comment. Inevitably others drew the conclusion that he was not actively supporting the King's policy and this must have disquieted Henry.

The recognition by the two Convocations of the King as Supreme Head of the Church of England in February 1531 would come as a shock to More. Again there is no record of his opinion, but he doubtless shared Bishop John Fisher's view that 'the fort is betrayed even of them that should have defended it'. The clergy finally submitted on 15 May 1532 and More resigned the Chancellorship on the following day. Some have seen a direct connection between the two events, but it was not as simple a matter

---

[1] To Cromwell. *Rogers*, No 199. This letter is of primary importance to an understanding of More's position. It is not an exception to his self-imposed silence on affairs of state. It was a confidential letter to the King's Secretary, and More would expect Cromwell to read it to the King, for whose ear it was obviously intended. A letter to the King (*Rogers*, No 198) of the same date refers to this letter to Cromwell. In it More begged the King not to be influenced against him by 'sinister information'.

to resign office in those days as in these; More had been negotiating through the Duke of Norfolk for permission to give up his office. His plea of ill health was not a diplomatic excuse, and he was probably glad to have such a good reason for withdrawing from public life. From then on the only comment recorded of his opinions (apart from the confidential letter to Cromwell) is given by Roper. When some of the bishops tried to persuade him to attend the coronation of Anne Boleyn on 1 June 1533, he declined their invitation and warned them that they were on a slippery slope; first would come the coronation, then they would be ordered to preach in its defence, and later to write books about it all. His own absence from the coronation must have angered the King and the new Queen. For a former Lord Chancellor to keep away from the ceremony was a marked action.

In his retirement More refused to form a party against the King, nor would he encourage anything in the nature of criticism. Even his own family did not know the true grounds of his views on public affairs. Eustace Chapuys, the Emperor's Ambassador, busied himself with schemes for defeating the King's policy, but he failed to draw Sir Thomas More into his net. He asked Chapuys not to visit him and he refused to touch a letter from the Emperor. If he read the letter, he would in duty be bound, he said, to show it to the King, and any hint that he was in touch with the Emperor 'might deprive him of the liberty he had always used in speaking boldly to King Henry'.

We may contrast this attitude with that taken up by Bishop John Fisher. He took counsel with Chapuys, who reported to the Emperor in September 1533 and again in

October that the Bishop would welcome armed intervention. Chapuys misread the temper of the times when he told his master that 'innumerable people from all ranks of society' would support such a venture. Had Chapuys's despatches been opened, Fisher could have been charged with treason and he would have had no defence other than that revolt against a tyrant is not sedition, an opinion approved by St Thomas Aquinas. Even in *Utopia* a prince or governor could be deposed if he showed signs of becoming a tyrant.[1]

More shared with his contemporaries the view that kingship was of divine origin and some of his references to Henry VIII may seem to us obsequious and only to be equalled, or surpassed, by Elizabethan courtiers and poets. There is no reason to think that More played the courtier; it would have been out of character for him to have so behaved. How, then, did it come about that this very loyal subject refused his consent to the King's wish in the matter of the Supremacy? It should be stressed that the measure of his allegiance is also the measure of the conviction that led him to withdraw his support on a matter of conscience. He might have felt safe in his retirement, for he had had the assurances of the King that his conscience would be respected. As he wrote to Cromwell in March 1534,[2] Henry had told him on his appointment as Chancellor in 1529, 'that he would in no wise that I should other thing do or say therein [i.e. the marriage question] than upon that that

---

[1] Those who condemn the Bishop for this conduct must also condemn Bishop Compton of London for signing the letter of invitation that brought William of Orange to England in 1688.

[2] *Rogers*, No 199.

London Bridge and the Tower in the XVIth century

I should perceive mine own conscience should serve me, and that I should first look unto God and after God unto him, which most gracious words were the first lesson that ever his Grace gave me at my first coming into his noble service [i.e. in 1517 as Councillor]'. Only a few months before More was sent to the Tower the King had included in his instructions to his ambassador to the Lutheran princes the sentence, 'though the law of every man's private conscience be but a poor court, yet it is the highest supreme court for judgment or justice'.[1] It was a noble sentiment that would have had More's approval, but he himself was not to be allowed to appeal to that 'highest supreme court'.

When Cranmer pronounced the marriage between Henry and Catherine to be invalid, Thomas More said to Roper, 'God give grace, son, that these matters within a while be not confirmed with oaths.' It was a prescient remark, for it was by this means that he was at last brought within the law. Other attacks failed; charges of corruption fell to the ground, and the attempt to indict him in the matter of the Nun of Kent was reluctantly abandoned by the King. The oath to the Succession proved the means to his ruin.

Though he would not state his reasons for refusing the oath, the Commissioners must have suspected why he did so. He was content to accept the line of succession: what was left? Two things: the declaration on the marriage, and the implied rejection of papal authority. Cromwell certainly knew the grounds of More's objection, for in the letter of March 1534 he had written to the Secretary on

[1] *L.P.*, Vol. 7, p. 58.

the Primacy of the Pope. 'In good faith I never neither read nor heard anything of such effect on the other side that ever could lead me to think that my conscience were well discharged, but rather in right great peril if I should follow the other side and deny the Primacy to be provided by God, which if we did, yet can I nothing perceive any commodity [advantage] that ever could come by that denial, for that Primacy is at leastwise instituted by the corps [whole body] of Christianity and for a great urgent cause in avoiding of schisms and corroborate by continual succession more than the space of a thousand years at the least. . . . And therefore *since all Christendom is one corps, I cannot perceive how any member thereof may without the common consent of the body depart from the common head.*' The italicized sentence gives the clue to Thomas More's opinion.

The Act of Succession had only just been passed by Parliament when More wrote those words, but the break with Rome had already been achieved. The acceptance by the Convocations of Henry as Supreme Head in 1531 and the passing of the Act of Restraint of Appeals by March 1533 had severed all links. The Abjuration of Papal Supremacy by the clergy a few weeks after More's letter confirmed what had already been effected as did the later Act of Supremacy of November 1534. A constitutional revolution had been carried out; King and Parliament had appropriated powers that had hitherto not been under secular regulation. Popes and kings had disagreed and quarrelled on matters that impinged on state authority, such as the appointments of bishops, appeals to Rome, taxation of the clergy, and so on, but no secular power had questioned the predominant spiritual jurisdiction of the Pope.

Thomas More had never dealt with this problem in his controversial writings. In these he had been concerned with the refutation of heresies and with defending the clergy. In his earlier years, with Colet and Erasmus, he had criticized the clergy both secular and regular, but when Lutheranism became a serious threat More felt that the more urgent need was to maintain the unity of the Church. The two pamphlets of Christopher Saint-German, *Spirituality and Temporality*, and *Salem and Bizance* to which More replied,[1] did not deal directly with the Primacy of the Pope. It was only after More had been committed to the Tower that Saint-German put forward his more radical views on Church and State.

One gets the impression that Parliament and, to a large extent, the clergy did not realize what a drastic change in the field of legislation had been carried out within a short period. The laity were intent on remedying abuses, some of them well founded, that affected their material condition; the clergy were warding off the anger of the King and of Parliament. Perhaps only Thomas Cromwell really saw the larger issues of the claim that 'this realm of England is an empire'. The change was far from being a simple transfer of powers; it involved difficult questions of spiritual authority. How far could a king, a layman, exercise as Supreme Head the spiritual functions of the Pope? It was to take many years before the problems could be resolved. The immediate result was that withdrawal from

[1] More was unaware of the anonymous author's identity with Saint-German.

the authority of the Pope was a break with the Universal Church, but of a different kind from that resulting from the Lutheran movement. Saint-German, in his pamphlet *An Answer to a Letter* (1535?), argued that Parliament and Convocation could not grant to the King authority over things 'mere spiritual'. Such a grant would have been void 'for they have no authority to change the law of God'. Thomas More would have agreed with his old opponent on this point, but he began further back with the Primacy of the Pope as of divine institution and therefore not subject to local legislation. He saw that repudiation of the authority of the Pope opened the door for schism, and schism would lead to heresy; as St Augustine had written, 'Heresy is schism grown old.'

It is difficult for us today to appreciate the horror with which heresy was regarded in the early part of the sixteenth century, and indeed for some time later. More had watched with consternation the rise and progress of Lutheranism; he had followed the growing dissensions in doctrine and discipline between such leaders as Zwingli, Oecolampadius and Bucer. Nearer home there had been William Tyndale and the younger 'reformers' such as Robert Barnes, Thomas Bilney and John Frith. With increasing dismay More read the books and pamphlets that were brought into the country or secretly printed and circulated. It was early in 1528 that Bishop Tunstall urged his old friend to combat heresy with his pen[1] and from then, until the pen was taken from his hand, he concentrated his thoughts on this duty that had been placed upon him. His direct dealings with heretics have been much

[1] *Rogers*, No 160.

discussed, and there is no need here to go over the ground again, save to note that the old charges of deliberate cruelty can no longer be sustained. In the Epitaph he composed about 1533 for the monument in Chelsea Old Church, he described himself as 'grievous to thieves, murderers and heretics'. In a letter to Erasmus[1] he stressed his antipathy to heretics. 'For I so entirely detest that race of men, that there is none to which I would be more hostile, unless they amend.' The Heresy Act of March 1534 must have deeply disturbed him and have stiffened his resolution to defend the Universal Church. It was not only that it imposed on bishops regulations for the trial of heretics, but it declared that 'no manner of speaking against the said Bishop of Rome or his pretended power . . . shall be deemed heresy'. It was further stated that the authority of the Pope 'was never commonly accepted or confirmed to be any law of God or man within this realm'. It is important that in assessing the significance of More's trial, we should keep in mind his continuous resistance to heresy. He was well aware of the need for reformation within the Church, just as he was well aware of the scandalous lives of some of the popes, but the greatest disaster to his mind would be the disruption of Christianity which must inevitably follow the denial of the Primacy of the Apostolic See. The only hope was to hold the Church together as 'one corps' under the Pope. The situation seemed to him desperate, as indeed it was, and only a united Church could effectively prevent the further spread of heresy.

Only a small group of men took up the same position. The bishops, save John Fisher, bowed to the King's will,

[1] *Allen*, 2831.

as did practically the whole body of the clergy. They acquiesced in the claim of King and Parliament to rule the Church as well as the State. Thomas More could not accept this revolutionary claim to complete national control of the Church. He approved of the limitations that had been imposed in the past on papal interference with purely temporal affairs, but he could not accept the right of any one member of the Universal Church to repudiate the spiritual authority of the Holy See. There he made his stand, and it was for the Primacy of the Pope and the Unity of the Church that he laid down his life.

Chapter 12

EXECUTION

IT is not proposed here to retell the story of Sir Thomas More's return to the Tower and of his last meeting with Margaret Roper and his son John. One or two points may be noted.

The journey was made down the river, but instead of going under London Bridge and so to Traitors' Gate, the barges were brought to the Old Swan stairs (now Old Swan Wharf) just above the Bridge. The narrowness of the arches and the size of the piers and starlings made the passage dangerous at flood and ebb tides. From the stairs the remainder of the journey was made on foot along Thames Street (now Lower Thames Street) to the Bulwark or western gate of the Tower. It was probably near this gate that Margaret and her brother waited for their father. Roper used the expression 'about the Tower Wharf'; the wharf itself was within the Tower. William Roper was surely there, as his account of the meeting is so charged with feeling that it suggests the record of an eyewitness.

Father Bridgett said that the tradition was that More was imprisoned in the Beauchamp Tower; this may be so, but it has not been possible to trace this tradition very far back. None of the early narratives give this information, nor did Cresacre More do so. Similarly the claim that John Fisher was imprisoned in the Bell Tower does not rest on early evidence.

The King made two concessions; the sentence on More of hanging at Tyburn was changed to beheading on Tower Hill, and his family had permission to be present

St Peter-ad-Vincula in the Tower

at his burial. More frankly admitted that he feared physical pain. He had written to Margaret, 'I am of nature so shrinking that I am almost afeared of a fillip [smart blow]', and to the priest Leder he wrote, 'If ever I should mishap me to receive the oath, ye may reckon sure that it were expressed and extorted by duress and hard handling. And I trust both that they will use no violent forcible ways, and also that if they would, God would give his grace, and the rather a great deal through good folks' prayers, give me strength to stand.' The last quotation hints at torture in the Tower, but the horrible butchery at Tyburn must often have been in his mind. As a commoner he was not entitled to the quick death of the axe.

When he was told that the King had granted that 'your wife, children and other friends shall have liberty to be present' at the burial, More replied, 'O how much beholden then am I to his Grace that unto my poor burial vouchsafeth to have so gracious consideration.' There was no sarcasm in those words; they were an expression of the honour More always paid to the office of king.

It may be hoped that he was unaware of the callous treatment of John Fisher's headless body which was left lying naked on the scaffold until the evening when it was taken by a soldier 'upon his halberd' to the churchyard of All Hallows, Barking, and there buried 'very contemptuously'.

The account of the execution in the *News Letter* was brief.

> The Wednesday [sic] following, he was beheaded in the great square in front of the Tower, and said little before execution only that the assistants should pray God for him and he would pray for them. Afterwards, he exhorted them and earnestly beseeched them to pray God for the King, so that He would give him good counsel, protesting that he died his good servant, but God's first.

The *Expositio* (this time rightly giving 'bonum consilium') added, 'Having thus spoken, with steadfast countenance, he placed his neck to receive the axe, not without a great moan from many.'

The next account, chronologically, was written by Edward Hall (d. 1547) in his *Chronicle*, first published in 1542. He had been appointed Common Serjeant to the City in 1532 and Under-Sheriff in 1535, and he may himself have been present at More's execution. The customary procedure was described by John Stow. 'Upon this Hill [Tower Hill] is always readily prepared at the charges of the City a large scaffold and gallows of timber, for the execution of such traitors or transgressors, as are delivered out of the Tower, or otherwise, to the Sheriffs of London by writ there to be executed.'[1] It would therefore not be surprising if Hall, as an Under-Sheriff, had been present on Tuesday, 6 July 1535; his official position would certainly make it possible for him to gather first-hand information. His account shows that as a staunch Henrician, he was inimical to More; this provides us with a view that must be taken into account as a contemporary opinion.

Also the 6th day of July was Sir Thomas More beheaded for the like treason before rehearsed, which as you have heard was for the denying the King's Majesty's Supremacy. This man was also counted learned, and as you have heard before he was Lord Chancellor of England, and in that time a great persecutor of such as detested the Supremacy of the Bishop of Rome, which he himself so highly favoured that he stood to it until he was brought to the scaffold on the Tower Hill where on a block his head was stricken off and

---

[1] Stow's *Survey* (ed. Kingsford), Vol. I, p. 129. On one occasion in the reign of Edward IV the Tower officials had carried out an execution on their own; when the Mayor protested, the King apologized.

had no more harm.[1] I cannot tell whether I should call him a foolish wise man, or a wise foolish man, for undoubtedly he beside his learning had a great wit, but it was so mingled with taunting and mockery that it seemed to them that best knew him, that he thought nothing to be well spoken except he had ministered some mock in the communication, insomuch as at his coming to the Tower, one of the officers demanded his upper garment for his fee, meaning his gown, and he answered he should have it and took off his cap, saying it was the uppermost garment that he had. Likewise, even going to his death at the Tower Gate, a poor woman called unto him and besought him to declare that he had certain evidences of hers in the time that he was in office (which after he was apprehended she could not come by) and that he would entreat she might have them again, or else she was undone. He answered, 'Good woman, have patience a little while, for the King is good unto me that even within this half hour he will discharge me of all my business, and help thee himself.' Also when he went up the stair on the scaffold, he desired one of the Sheriff's officers to give him his hand to help him up, and said, 'When I come down again, let me shift for myself as well as I can.' Also the hangman kneeled down to him asking him forgiveness of his death (as the manner is) to whom he said, 'I forgive thee, but I promise thee that thou shalt never have honesty [credit] of the striking off my head, my neck is so short.' Also even when he should lay down his head on the block, he having a great gray beard, striked out his beard and said to the hangman, 'I pray you let me lay my beard over the block lest ye should cut it'; thus with a mock he ended his life.[2]

[1] In a letter to Margaret (*Rogers*, No 210), More had written, 'it is a case in which a man may lose his head and yet have none harm'. Perhaps it was a current saying.

[2] *Henry VIII* (ed. Whibley), Vol. II, p. 265.

Harpsfield seems to have used Hall for the incident of the poor woman, and then to have incorporated Roper's account. Both are at fault in speaking of 'Master Lieutenant'; here Hall wrote with the authority of a City official; the duties of the Lieutenant of the Tower ended when he had handed over his prisoner.[1]

When he was thus passing to his death, a certain woman called to him at the Tower gate, beseeching him to notify and declare that he had certain evidences of hers that were delivered to him when he was in office, saying that after he was once apprehended, she could not come by them, and that he would entreat that she might recover her said evidences again, the loss of which would import her utter undoing. 'Good woman,' quoth he, 'content thyself, and take patience a little while, for the King is so good and gracious to me, that even within this half-hour he will disburden me of all worldly business, and help thee himself.'

When he was going up to the scaffold, which was so weak that it was ready to fall, he said merrily to Master Lieutenant, 'I pray you, Master Lieutenant, see me safe up, and for my coming down let me shift for myself.'

Then desired he all the people thereabouts to pray for him, and to bear witness with him that he should now there suffer death in and for the faith of the Holy Catholic Church. Which done, he kneeled down, and after his prayers said, turned to the executioner, and with a cheerful countenance spake thus unto him, 'Pluck up thy spirits, man, and be not afraid to do thine office; my neck is very short; take heed therefore thou strike not awry, for saving of thine honesty.'

So passed Sir Thomas More out of this world to God, upon the very same day in which himself had most desired.

[1] The senior Sheriff who received More from the Lieutenant was Humphrey Monmouth, the patron of William Tyndale.

It will be noted that Harpsfield and Roper omitted the words recorded in the *News Letter*: 'he died his good servant, but God's first'. They included, what is not given in the *News Letter*, More's declaration that he suffered 'death in and for the faith of the Holy Catholic Church'.

We can now turn to Stapleton's *Tres Thomae* for the first time, as it gives additional information which he derived from John Harris and his wife Dorothy Colley. Stapleton was intimate with both of them at Louvain and Douai; Harris died in 1579, but his widow was still alive in the 1580s, when *Tres Thomae* was being written. She must have been very old then, but we must not assume that what Stapleton recorded were the memories of an old woman. He had known her for thirty years, and, it will be seen, he also drew upon the recollections of Margaret Giggs (d. 1570) and of her husband John Clement (d. 1572). One would like to know when Stapleton wrote down these various stories of More's last days; was he, in 1588, trusting to his own memory, or had he by him his notes taken in earlier years? Here is his account of the execution.

When the day arrived which was to bring to More death, or rather life, he was led out of his prison. His beard was long and disordered, his face was pale and thin from the rigour of his confinement. He held in his hand a red cross and raised his eyes to heaven. His robe was of the very poorest and coarsest. He had decided to make his last journey in a better garment and to put on the gown of camlet which Bonvisi had given him in prison, both to please his friend and to be able to give it to the executioner. But through the avarice or wickedness of his gaoler, he, so great and renowned, he who had held such high office, went out clad in his servant's gown made of the basest material that we call frieze.

Harpsfield, after Roper, gave a different account of this gown incident.

Upon whose departure, Sir Thomas More, as one that had been invited to some solemn feast, changed into his best apparel; which Master Lieutenant espying, advised him to put it off, saying that he that should have it was but a javel.[1] *'What, Master Lieutenant,' quoth he, 'should I account him a javel that shall do me this day so singular a benefit? Nay, I assure you, were it cloth of gold, I would account it well bestowed on him, as St Cyprian did, who gave to his executioner thirty pieces of gold.' And albeit at length, through Master Lieutenant's importunate persuasion, he altered his apparel, yet after the example of that Holy Martyr Saint Cyprian, did he, of that little money that was left him, send one angel of gold to his executioner, and so was he by Master Lieutenant brought out of the Tower, and from thence toward the place of execution.*

Stapleton continued:

Margaret Giggs, the wife of John Clement, once showed me a life-like image [picture?], made with great skill, of More going out to the place of execution, and in accordance with that image I have here described his appearance and demeanour. She was present at More's death and assisted the other Margaret, Roper's wife, to bury him.

As he was passing on his way, a certain woman offered him wine, but he refused it, saying, 'Christ in his passion was given not wine but vinegar to drink.'

Another woman shouted at him and demanded to know what he had done with certain documents which she had

[1] Low fellow.

entrusted to him while he was Chancellor. 'Good woman,' he replied, 'as for your documents, have patience, I beseech you, for the space of one short hour. For then from the care of your documents and from every other burden, the King's Majesty in his goodness will give me complete relief.'

He was again interrupted by another woman, who perhaps felt that she had a grievance or perhaps was suborned by others, and now cried out that he had done her a grave injury while he was Chancellor. 'I remember your case quite well,' he gravely replied, 'and if I had to pass sentence again, it would be just the same as before.'

At an earlier place in his book, Stapleton told the story of 'a certain citizen of Winchester'[1] who had sought More's advice in a period of temptation. His spiritual troubles returned to him, so he went up to London in the hope of again consulting More, but this was impossible during the imprisonment.

On More's way, then, from the Tower to the scaffold he burst through the guards and cried out with a loud voice, 'Do you recognize me, Sir Thomas? Help me, I beg you: for that temptation has returned to me and I cannot get rid of it.' More at once answered, 'I recognize you perfectly. Go and pray for me, and I will pray earnestly for you.' He went away, and never again in his whole life was he troubled with such temptations.

We return to Stapleton's main narrative.

When he arrived at the place of execution and was about to mount the scaffold, he stretched out his hand for

---

[1] More was a Justice of the Peace for Hampshire and must have been at Winchester in the course of his duties.

assistance, saying, 'I pray you, see me safe up, and for my coming down let me shift for myself.' On the scaffold he wished to speak to the people, but was forbidden to do so by the Sheriff. He contented himself therefore with saying: 'I call to witness, brothers, that I die the faithful servant of God and the King, and in the faith of the Catholic Church.' . . . After kneeling down, he recited aloud the Psalm, 'Have mercy on me, O God.' . . . After saying the Psalm and finishing his prayer, he rose briskly, and when, according to custom, the executioner begged his pardon, he kissed him with great love, gave him a gold angel-noble and said to him, 'Thou wilt give me this day a greater benefit than ever any mortal man can be able to give me. Pluck up thy spirits, man, and be not afraid to do thine office. My neck is very short: take heed, therefore, thou strike not awry for saving of thine honesty [credit].' . . . Then the executioner wished to bind his eyes, but he said, 'I will cover them myself.' He covered his face with a linen cloth he had brought with him, and joyfully and calmly laid his head on the block: it was at once struck off.[1]

Hall and Harpsfield recorded the incident of one woman; Stapleton added two women and the man from Winchester. There may be some duplication here, but it is impossible to determine what exactly happened during that walk from the Tower Gate to Tower Hill, a matter of some two hundred yards. Stapleton's narrative must be read with some reservation. If, for instance, we compare his account of More's defence at the trial, it will be seen that he did a certain amount of rewriting to underline some of the points. His description of the execution, however, owed something to the recollections of Margaret

[1] *Stapleton*, pp. 71, 208–211.

Giggs, who was present, and this gives it a special value.

Both John Fisher and Thomas More died without the presence of any relative or friend. More was probably unaware that Margaret Giggs was in the crowd that always thronged Tower Hill on such occasions. He would know that his daughter Margaret would be somewhere near, waiting to carry out her last sad duty to him. Accounts of other executions tell of relatives and friends accompanying the doomed man; sometimes, indeed, the scaffold must have been uncomfortably crowded. Nothing is said of a priest or even a servant being with Fisher or More. We always think of Thomas More as the centre of a very lively family circle and of a multitude of friends. The King kept the family away from the execution and he may have refused permission for any friend to be there. Perhaps they dared not be there. Thomas More died a lonely man separated from all those he loved. He himself may have willed it that way.

Chapter 13

THE BURIAL

NEITHER Roper nor Harpsfield gave any particulars of
the burial. For these we have to rely on Stapleton.

His body was buried by Margaret Roper and Margaret
Clement in the little Chapel of St Peter-in-the-Tower, by
permission of the Lieutenant. In regard to this burial an
incident occurred which may well be regarded as miraculous.
Margaret Roper from earliest morning had been going from
church to church and distributing such generous alms to the
poor that her purse was now empty. After her father's
execution she hastened to the Tower to bury his body, for
the Lieutenant had promised to allow this with the permission of the King, which was readily given. In her hurry she
forgot to replenish her purse and found that she had no
winding sheet for the body. She was in the greatest distress
and knew not what to do. Her maid Dorothy, afterwards
Mrs Harris, suggested that she should get some linen from
a neighbouring shop. 'How can I do that,' she answered,
'when I have no money left?' 'They will give you credit,'
replied the maid. 'I am far away from home,' said Margaret,
'and no one knows me here, but yet go and try.' The maid
went into a neighbouring shop and asked for as much linen
as was needed: she agreed on the price. Then she put her hand
into her purse as if to look for money, intending to say that
unexpectedly she found herself without money, but that if
the shopkeeper would trust her she would obtain the price

of the linen as quickly as possible from her mistress and bring it back. But although the maid was quite certain that she had absolutely no money, yet in her purse she found exactly the price of the linen, not one farthing more nor less than the amount she had agreed to pay. Dorothy Harris, who is still living in Douai, has told me these details again and again. With this winding sheet, so strangely obtained, the two Margarets and Dorothy most reverently buried the body.[1]

St Peter-ad-Vincula[2] is squeezed between the western inner wall of the Tower and the buildings that are now the Waterloo Barracks. It is a small chapel only sixty-five feet long. The present northern wall dates from the times of Edward I. A fire early in the sixteenth century destroyed most of the chapel and it was rebuilt early in the reign of Henry VIII. There were two altars, one of St Peter and the other of Our Lady. The main entrance is at the western end, where there is a miniature belfry. The first to be buried within the chapel after rebuilding was the Earl of Kildare, who died a prisoner within the Tower in December 1534. The second burial was that of Sir Thomas More. The Chapel was the burial-place of many of those executed on Tower Hill or on Tower Green. Macaulay wrote:

> In truth there is no sadder spot on earth than that little cemetery. Death is there associated, not, as in Westminster Abbey and Saint Paul's, with genius and virtue, with public veneration and with imperishable renown; not, as in our

[1] *Stapleton*, p. 213.
[2] The only other church so dedicated is in Rome. 'St Peter-where-the-chains-are' is an appropriate dedication for a chapel in a prison.

humblest churches and churchyards, with everything that
is most endearing in social and domestic charities; but with
whatever is darkest in human nature and human destiny,
with the savage triumph of implacable enemies, with the
inconstancy, the ingratitude, the cowardice of friends,
with all the miseries of fallen greatness and of blighted fame.
Thither have been carried, through successive ages, by the
rude hands of gaolers, without one mourner following, the
bleeding relics of men who had been captains of armies, the
leaders of parties, the oracles of senates, and the ornaments
of courts.[1]

Macaulay added a footnote:

I cannot refrain from expressing my disgust at the barbarous stupidity which has transformed this most interesting
little church into the likeness of a meeting-house in a manu-
facturing town.

He was writing in the middle of last century. By then the
Chapel had been packed with box-pews and a two-decker
pulpit and a gallery had been added. It had become the
parish church for the Tower and many of the inhabitants
were buried beneath its floor.

It was decided in 1876 to carry out a complete 'restoration'. The first problem was how to level the floor, which
had become very uneven owing to the sinking of the
ground due to the many burials. The clerk of the com-
mittee that supervised the work wrote:[2] 'On removing
the stones of the pavement it was found that the resting-
places of those who had been buried within the walls of

---

[1] *History*, Vol. I, p. 479.
[2] D. C. Bell, *St Peter-ad-Vincula* (1877).

the Chapel . . . had been repeatedly and it was feared almost universally desecrated.' Most of the burials had been only two or three feet below the floor and to say that the space was overcrowded is an understatement. Burials had gone on for more than three hundred years. The report stated that, 'all the human remains which were found beneath the floor were carefully collected and enclosed in boxes and removed to the crypt'. Strictly speaking, there was no crypt; the bones were placed in a vault to the north of the Chapel. Greater care was taken with burials near the altar of St Peter, as it was believed that this part had been used mainly for royalty or those of ducal rank, but here, too, the ground was 'much disturbed and many bones missing'. The identification of these remains is very doubtful, but the bones were sorted out, and, to use the clerk's language, 'these several parcels were duly labelled and fastened up'. They were later coffined and reburied in marked places.

Cresacre More said that Thomas More was buried 'in the belfry or, as some say, as one entereth into the vestry'. The belfry is an impossible site, as it is almost completely filled with the stone stairs. The words 'as some say, as one entereth into the vestry' were not in the original manuscript. There was, however, as the clerk noted, 'an inconvenient wooden structure near the west entrance door' which was pulled down during the restoration. It seems likely then that the body of Sir Thomas More was buried near the west door. The *Grey Friars' Chronicle*[1] recorded that the body of John Fisher was removed from All Hallows churchyard and reburied near that of Sir

[1] *Grey Friars' Chronicle* (Camden Society), p. 38.

Thomas More. Today their bones are mingled with others in the vault.

John Fisher's head was removed from London Bridge and thrown into the river to be replaced by that of Sir Thomas More. The story of how Margaret Roper by bribery managed to save her father's head is well known. During her lifetime (she died in 1544) the head remained in her care. It is said that she left it to her eldest daughter, Lady Elizabeth Bray, who died in 1558. Stapleton,[1] presumably on the authority of Dorothy Colley, stated that 'to this day it [the head] remains in the custody of one of his relatives'. Cresacre More,[2] writing about 1630, stated that Margaret Roper buried the head 'where she thought fittest'. The next reference comes in John Aubrey's *Brief Lives*,[3] which was compiled round about 1680. He wrote that the head 'is now preserved in the cathedral church [sic] at Canterbury'. Edward Hasted in his *County of Kent*[4] stated that the Roper vault in St Dunstan's Church, Canterbury, had been closed up, as it was 'very full'; he continued, 'In a hollow in the wall of the vault underneath, having an iron grate before it, next to the coffin of the above Margaret, there is still remaining a skull, being that of Sir Thomas More.' He was mistaken in saying that Margaret Roper was buried in the Roper vault.[5]

A correspondent wrote in *The Gentleman's Magazine* in May 1837:

In the chancel [sic] of the church is a vault belonging to

[1] *Stapleton*, p. 213.
[2] *Life*, p. 289.
[3] *Lives* (ed. Powell), p. 317.
[4] 1799 edition, Vol. IX, p. 37.
[5] *See* above, p. 12.

the [Roper] family which, in newly paving the chancel in the summer of 1835, was accidentally opened; and, wishing to ascertain whether Sir Thomas More's skull was really there, I went down into the vault and found it still remaining in the place where it was seen many years ago, in a niche in the wall, in a leaden box, something of the shape of a bee-hive, open in the front and with an iron grating before it.

The vault was beneath the Roper Chantry (founded 1402), now the Chapel of St Nicholas. A tablet was set in the floor in 1932 with this inscription:

BENEATH THIS FLOOR
IS THE VAULT OF THE
ROPER FAMILY IN WHICH
IS INTERRED THE HEAD OF
SIR THOMAS MORE
OF ILLUSTRIOUS MEMORY
SOMETIME LORD CHANCELLOR
OF ENGLAND WHO WAS
BEHEADED ON TOWER HILL
6th JULY 1535
ECCLESIA ANGLICANA LIBERA SIT

APPENDIX

CONVERSATION BETWEEN SIR THOMAS MORE AND
SIR RICHARD RICH, 12 JUNE 1535

Reference: P.R.O., S.P.2/R, folios 24 and 25. *Letters and Papers,
Henry VIII,* Vol. 8, No. 814, 2, ii.

N.B. The series of dots indicates only roughly the extent of the
lacunae.

[f.24.] The effect of the . . . between Rychard . . . / and
the sayd Sir Thomas More in the presence of . . . / Edmund
Walsyngham Rychard Southewell / [*blank*] Palmer and
[*blank*] Berleght.
. . . . charitably movyd the seyd Sir Thomas More to be
conformable / . . . . lawes as wer made concernyng the case
that he knew of / upon condycion that yf the seyd More wold
so be that he wold . . . on his / [f. 25.] . . . . to whome the
seyd More gave thanks saying that your cons. . . . . / Save
you and my conscience shall save me. Wheruppon the seyd
Rychard / . . . to the seyd More Sir for me to gyve you
advyse or counsell beyng a / . . . experyence lernyng &
wysedome yt were lyke as yf a man wold take / . . . . of
water and cast yt in to Temmys by cause yt shold not be /
. . . Sir protestyng with you that I have no commission or
commaundment to / . . . of the mater ye wott of Nevertheless with your favour I ask / . . . you this case If it were
inactyd by Parlyament that I should be King / . . . and who
so ever sayd nay .t.d. what offence were yt to y . . . / If

ye seyd h . . . I were King for sothe . . . my consayence
yt werre none off . . / . . . ye were bound to say and to .
ccept me for so muche as your consent / . . . . . . wherunto
. . . seyd More sayd that he should offende . . / . . . . . for
he . . . bound by the act by cause he myght gyve his / . . . .
And he sayd further . . . t the same case was a . . . case /
. . . . putt a nother hyer case whiche was this Sir I put
case / . . . . . by Parlyament that god were not god And
if any Repug . . . / same act that yt shold be treson yf the
questyon were askyd of your . . . / . . . ye say that god
were . . t god according to the Statute And if he dyd, dyd /
you offende yea for sothe wherunto the seyd Ryche sayd that
act was not / possyble to be made to make god ungod but
Sir by cause your case is . . . . . / . . . to you & me . . . .
ys Syr . . . to be pl. . . . . Ingland. . . . .
. . . . . / . . . affirme & accept . . so as welle as in the case
that I were made Kyng . . . / . . iche case ye agre that ye
were bound so to affirme & accept me to be Kyng . . . / . . . .
erunto the seyd More sayd that the cases were not lyke by cause
that a Kyng / . . . y be made by parlyament and a Kyng
depryved by Parlyament to whiche act any / . . . Subyettes
beyng of the parlyament may gyve his concent but to the case
/ . . . . a Subyett can not be bound by cause he cannot gyve
his cause . . / . . . hym . . . Parlyiament Saying further
that although the Kyng were acceptyd / in Ingland yet moste
Utter partes doo not affirme the same Whereunto the sayd /
Ryche sayd Well Sir god comfort you for I see your mynd
wyll not change / which I fere wyll be very daungerous to
you for I suppose your concelement to the / questyon that
hath been askyd of you as high offence as other that hath . . . .
/ and thus Jesu send you better grace

Index